A Song of Faith and Hope

A Song of Faith and Hope

The Life of Frankie Muse Freeman

by Frankie Muse Freeman
with Candace O'Connor

Missouri Historical Society Press
distributed by University of Missouri Press

Published in the United States of America by Missouri Historical Society Press
P.O. Box 11940, St. Louis, Missouri 63112-0040

07 06 05 04   2 3 4 5

Library of Congress Cataloging-in-Publication Data

Freeman, Frankie Muse, 1916–
A Song of faith and hope : the life of Frankie Muse Freeman / by Frankie Muse
Freeman, with Candace O'Connor.
           p. cm.
Includes index.
ISBN 1-883982-41-3 (cloth : alk. paper)

1. Freeman, Frankie Muse, 1916– 2. Lawyers—United States—Biography. 3.
Civil Rights—United States—History. I. O'Connor, Candace. II. Title
           KF373.F746A3 2003
           340'.092—dc21

                                                                    2002155356

Distributed by University of Missouri Press
Design by Robyn Morgan
Cover design by artist Lucy Josey, who is a painter, weaver, dress designer, and
professor in Howard University's fashion program.

Printed and bound in Canada by Friesens

∞ the paper used in this publication meets minimum requirements of the ANSI/NISO Z39.48-1992 (R
1997) (Permanence of Paper).

Cover: Frankie Freeman on the steps of the St. Louis Federal Courthouse with
NAACP attorney Constance Baker Motley, October 1954.

Whatever I may have accomplished in my life
as reflected in this book
would not have been possible
without the encouragement, help, and support
of many people,
especially my parents and husband,
to whom I am especially indebted,
and I dedicate this book to them.

Contents

Foreword

Some years ago, I was Frankie Freeman's guest at her Muse family reunion held at the Brooklyn home of her newly wed, talented daughter, Pat. I enjoyed the hospitality reminiscent of my native Virginia, which I had left in my childhood. But it was the warmth of relationships and the camaraderie that made me feel embraced in a family as loving as my own. I felt a kinship. In retrospect, as I read her book, I see the similarities in the do's and don'ts, the value messages, and the culture and personal expectations in the shaping of our lives.

Attorney Freeman is deeply rooted in her family values, and her story shows how one balances a career and family life. The support of her husband and family enabled her to travel extensively in the quest for civil rights. In the midst of all her highly visible community and national involvement, she easily could have written a great cookbook from her own kitchen. Even when she traveled, wherever she was, she carried a variety of food. At conferences and especially at sorority conventions, many knew to gather in her room for the best of her home-cooked morsels.

Frankie was a pioneer as an African American woman in the field of law, and a barrier breaker in many other areas. Her book is testimony to what can be done when one believes passionately that achieving women's rights is essential to achieving racial justice. She does not hesitate to challenge forces directed toward depriving people of their rights and the meeting of basic needs—food, clothing, and decent housing.

Frankie's knowledge and appreciation of tradition and historic values have not held her hostage to the past. Rather, with due respect, she is ever open to what is creative and good. When faced with the impossible, she draws on her faith and ingenuity to find new strategies, new resources, and ultimate solutions. She demonstrates the perspective of a realist who sees the positive over the negative and, in her own way, cultivates the positive.

Appointed by President Lyndon B. Johnson as the first woman on the U.S. Commission on Civil Rights, Frankie served with distinction for an unprecedented sixteen years. In hearings across the country, she was buoyed by her respect for people of all backgrounds, her faith, and her drive for justice. Likewise, with her commitment and activism focus, as national president she rallied the members of Delta Sigma Theta, a public-service sorority, around the theme of "One Nation or Two." This deep devotion to civil and human rights is reflected throughout her career—whatever the price she paid.

Mary McLeod Bethune, founder of the National Council of Negro Women (NCNW), wrote in her last will and testament, "Faith is the first factor in a life dedicated to service. Without it, nothing is possible. With it, nothing is impossible." I am often reminded of that when I think of Frankie, all she was able to do, and the injustices she confronted and overturned. In the height of the civil rights movement, she braved rural Mississippi to investigate the bombings of four black churches; it was at a time when several civil rights workers had been murdered for trying to register blacks to vote. I remember well the situation, for it was around that same time I traveled with two groups of northern black and white women, who under NCNW's "Wednesdays in Mississippi" went into a tense and segregated Mississippi to support Bob Moses and the Freedom Schools. Lest we forget, this book is a reminder of the courage of the many who risked their lives with faith for the progress that was to come.

Frankie Freeman walks the walk. She chose to take an active hand for the betterment of others; she is living proof that doing so gives one inner strength. She has the special knack of being able to operate in the now as she contemplates the future. She is ever current on civil, social, and political issues and remains available to share her cogent perspective.

Read *A Song of Faith and Hope* and witness the wide range of her work in public and private agencies as a professional or a volunteer, as an officer or a member, as an employee or a presidential appointee, as a leader or a participant, as a local or a national leader, and note a remarkable record of achievement against the odds. Find out how complex government agencies, not-for-profit nongovernmental community-service or national organizations, carry out their missions. See how it is that a highly qualified professional relates and serves people in all walks of life. Get a sense of what it takes not only to serve but also to work to empower people. Feel the sense of commitment and the strength of a woman dedicated to civil and human rights. Enjoy the musings of a friend who is just plain fun. Share the many honors and accolades of one for whom excellence means doing even ordinary tasks extraordinarily well. Inform, inspire, and encourage individuals, established leaders, and new generations of leadership with this book rich with learnings shared by my dear sister friend of more than forty years, my soror Frankie Muse Freeman.

—DOROTHY I. HEIGHT
President of the National Council of Negro Women

Foreword

Frankie Muse Freeman has had an interesting life. That fact alone makes *A Song of Faith and Hope* a valuable addition to the publications of the Missouri Historical Society Press.

But Ms. Freeman's autobiography is more than just a story to enjoy. Her story is one we can use as a measure of the past against which to examine our present and map out our future. Have we as individuals and as a society accomplished all that we can to make a better world for those who come after us? How can we build that better future and correct mistakes of the past? These are surely questions that Frankie Freeman in her long career has asked herself. That career of accomplishment, of faith and hope, is a standard we can well apply.

The values that Frankie Freeman's family embedded in her—empathy, respect, good manners, a strong work ethic, and the importance of education, of family, and of neighborhood—are timeless, relevant to any place and anyone's own story. Her parents were not blind to ignorance and prejudice but taught her appropriate ways to combat such obstacles, lessons she remembered even when confronted with the hatred and violence that grew out of that ignorance. Her contributions in a battle that has not yet entirely been won are an example of positive action that speaks to us all.

In *A Song of Faith and Hope* we recognize stories from America's immediate past: school segregation, unfair housing practices, President Lyndon Johnson's U.S. Commission on Civil Rights, politics in St. Louis. We hear them from what may be a new perspective, that of an African American woman in the midst of these issues and events. We learn, too, personal details of Ms. Freeman's story, her joys and tragedies, her patience and strength—her faith and hope.

As Ms. Freeman concludes the story of her life thus far, she takes note of the importance of "pride in diversity" but writes that we can't really take pride in our diversity until we get to know one another, and we have to work at that. Thanks, Frankie Freeman, for letting us know you a little better, for helping us take pride in a woman of St. Louis, a woman of faith and hope.

—ROBERT R. ARCHIBALD
President, Missouri Historical Society

Acknowledgments

First, I want to acknowledge the invaluable role of Candace O'Connor, who served as collaborator for this book. Also, thanks to scholar Gary Kremer, who reviewed the work in progress and made suggestions; Victoria Thomas, who served as research assistant; and Lucy Josey, who designed the front cover. Gloria Waters White gave continuous support and encouragement and helped me bring order to my files in preparation for the book. The many who reviewed the manuscript and made suggestions included my daughter, Shelbe "Pat" Bullock, my cousin Constance Morris Hope, Maxine and James Pyant, Cynthia and Ronald Thompson, Pauline Payne, and Margie Hollins. My sister, Allie Muse Peeples, and brothers William "Bill" Muse and Andrew "Andy" Muse helped jog my memory concerning a few early dates and events. In addition, I acknowledge with deep appreciation Dr. Dorothy I. Height and Dr. Robert Archibald for writing the forewords. Further thanks to Linda Connor; Janice Mosby; Ina Boon; Allen Fisher, archivist at the Lyndon B. Johnson Library in Austin, Texas; Rita and Thad Hollie; and Stephanie Chatman-Adkins. Finally, thanks to my friends and family for their encouragement and "push" when I felt like giving up.

Introduction

A Song of Faith and Hope
The Life of Frankie Muse Freeman

Today, many Americans cannot remember a time when African American children had to grow up in communities where they could not ride in the front of a bus, eat a hot dog at a lunch counter downtown, spend the night with their parents in a motel, or sit in a classroom with other children whose skin happened to be white. They learned early on that they could be turned away from hospitals and libraries, parks, playgrounds, and movie theaters.

I know very well that these things happened, because I lived with them daily during my childhood in Danville, Virginia, which was part of the "Jim Crow" South. I could not ride in the front of the streetcar, I could not go to local movie theaters unless I sat high up in the balcony, and I went to a school where all the other children had the same skin color that I did. But my family and I resisted as much as we could. Instead of riding the streetcar, for example, we chose to walk everywhere we went.

From an early age, I knew that I wanted to do something about this kind of discrimination, and somehow the law seemed like the route for me to follow. Maybe it was because a relative of mine had married a lawyer; maybe it was because I was always assertive, with strong opinions, and did not mind a fight. Maybe it was the example of what the law can do, for good and for ill. I was well aware of the *Plessy v. Ferguson* decision—handed down only twenty years before I was born—which made the pernicious "separate but equal" doctrine the law of the land; on the other hand, I also knew about the ringing dissent of Justice John M. Harlan, who declared that the Constitution was colorblind and that, in regard to civil rights, all citizens were equal before the law.

These promises of the Constitution gave me hope for change. During my undergraduate years at Hampton Institute, I decided to become a lawyer; at Howard University School of Law, surrounded by role models such as Spottswood Robinson and Thurgood Marshall, I decided to focus on civil rights. I also made up my mind to concentrate on litigation, a difficult and unusual field for any woman then. I took my first civil rights case in 1949, participated in many others, and in 1964 was appointed to the U.S. Commission on Civil Rights. In my professional work and many volunteer positions, I have made civil rights and the struggle against "isms"—racism, sexism, and ageism—the mission of my life.

As I have traveled across this country, I have been concerned about the gap between preachment and practice. Most Americans still need to understand that our nation will always be in trouble until they do more than pay lip service to civil rights. I have tried to do that in my own career, throughout many court cases and many commission hearings. I feel fortunate to have had these opportunities for service.

All the while, I never worked in a vacuum. I had a husband and two children, one of them with serious disabilities; I was a lawyer when few women and fewer black women were lawyers. Always, I tried to strike a balance: being a good wife, good mother, good lawyer, and good federal official. Always, I was undergirded by faith, hope, and constant prayers— "Help me, Lord," "Thank you, Lord." I also had the lessons I learned from my parents and teachers to give me strength, such as "Keep your chin up," "Keep smiling," "Do your homework," and "Do your job."

Things have changed in many ways since those Jim Crow days. Yet, after all these years, there are still more battles to be fought. As a society, we need to guard against racial, gender, and age discrimination; attacks on affirmative action; lack of access to health care; and racial isolation in housing, which also leads to educational inequality. But I remain optimistic about the future: I believe that the same faith and hope that have sustained me will continue to support those who engage in these struggles for justice. As James Weldon Johnson wrote in the "Negro National Anthem," which I learned in my early childhood:

> Sing a song full of the faith that the dark past has taught us,
> Sing a song full of the hope that the present has brought us,
> Facing the rising sun of our new day begun
> Let us march on till victory is won.

A Song of Faith and Hope

Chapter One

Well with My Soul
Growing Up in Danville
1916–33

I WAS BORN MARIE FRANKIE MUSE. My sister still calls me Marie when she wants to get my attention, but I actually dropped that name when I got married. All my life, I have been called Frankie, and at times that has been confusing to people. Even now, I get letters at my law office addressed to "Mr. Frankie Freeman." I do not hurry to write those people back.

I am named for my grandfather, Frank Muse, a tobacco farmer in Penhook, Franklin County, Virginia, whom I remember well. As a child, I never heard stories about slavery in my family, but I took it for granted that my great-grandparents were slaves. All my ancestors, on the maternal and paternal side, were connected in some way with white folks. We are all colors in my family. In Virginia, there are black Muse families and white Muse families, all related.

Some years ago, my brother Andrew, who is a lawyer, was trying a criminal case in Franklin County before a judge named Hopkins, which is a name on my paternal grandmother's side of the family. During the trial the judge interrupted the proceedings and asked to see counsel. When my brother went in to talk to him, he said, "Aren't you Frank Muse's grandson?" Andy said yes, and the judge replied: "I know you. We're cousins." The judge was white. Any number of times in the South, and particularly in Virginia, you knew there was some relationship, but that never bothered anyone. It may be difficult for people who are not southerners

Frankie as a baby, 1917.

to understand that, in spite of the racial segregation of the time, there was sometimes a closeness there.

You could see both sides of things in the town where I was born: Danville, Virginia, the last capital of the Confederacy, located very near the North Carolina border. It was a small town, about thirty thousand people then, but I did not think of it as being small or large or anything—just Danville, a typical southern town, and a center where the tobacco grown in that region was measured, bought, and sold. There was also the Dan River cotton mill, which manufactured beautiful fabric, as I remember.

Our family lived at 215 Ross Street, two blocks off Main. On the 200 and 300 blocks of Ross, the families were black, on both sides of the street. To go downtown, my sisters, brothers, and I had to walk past the houses in the 100 block of Ross, where the families were all white. As we passed by, the white children playing in the yards would often smile and say in an undertone, "nigger, nigger, nigger." We smiled back and responded, "cracker, cracker, cracker." Nobody frowned, and no voices were raised; the white children kept on playing, and we kept on walking. Meanwhile, the white parents, sitting on their porches, probably thought to themselves how peaceful it was—so nice and quiet. Then, when we wanted to have our shoes repaired, the children in my family would take them to a shop in the basement of a white man, Mr. Wrigley, who lived near the end of the 100 block. When the shoes were ready, his children would deliver them to our house. Those were the kinds of things that happened daily.

We also spoke to everyone we passed on the street, white or black. If you were polite, you always said, "Good morning." It was not a matter of race; it was a question of manners. Years later, when I went to New York City, I was walking down the street with my Aunt D saying "Good morning" to everyone, and she chided me, "What's *wrong* with you, Frankie? You don't do that in New York." But even now, when I get on an elevator, I say, "Good morning" or "Good afternoon." Some people respond, and some glance at me sideways, but I still do it.

If you are not from the South, you don't have a clue as to how it was. In St. Louis, for example, there was segregation by neighborhood, but in some places in the South back then, you had unwritten rules of segregation by block, sometimes even by the *side* of the block. As time went on, the system became more rigid, but you always knew exactly how and with whom you could socialize. Yet, strange as it may seem, we were actually closer—we knew each other better there, black and white—than we did in New York. There was a coldness in the North—not the kind of empathy, the kind of humanity, that I grew up with in my neighborhood in Danville.

My Grandparents

In Franklin County, there is a place called Museville, which shows that there were a lot of Muses in the area. My grandfather Frank Muse, who lived about ten miles from Museville, was one of them. He was a businessman and tobacco farmer who also raised hogs and kept cows for milk. Everybody in that area, black or white, called him "Uncle Frank." As a young man, he had known Booker T. Washington, who was born in Franklin County. There is now a Booker T. Washington Highway and memorial in the area that my family and I still visit when we hold family reunions in Danville.

Some outsiders have the perception that, in those days, all black folks were poor, but that is not true. My grandfather was a strong person and a successful one, who had managed to acquire a lot of property; his farm was mechanized long before a lot of others in that area. At one point, the highway department put State Route 40 through the center of the state, and Frank Muse sold them some of his property. Once the road was cut, he still owned land on both sides of the road. When merchants from the town of Penhook wanted to relocate to the main highway, he sold them some of that land for their businesses and also for the Penhook post office.

You did not mess with Frank Muse—he "didn't catch no stuff," people said—no matter what color you were. One time some men in sheets, probably from the Ku Klux Klan, came onto his property. The story goes that he shot the horses out from under them and ran up and told them to get those dead horses off his land; then, still not content, he went looking for them. A lot of times when I was growing up and had been disobedient, I would be accused of being "just like your grandfather."

Every summer we spent a couple weeks at his big, two-story white farmhouse on the hill with its double porches, upstairs and down. Because I was named for my grandfather and also was the oldest child, some people in my family felt that I was his favorite. I certainly have fond memories of him, though he was hard on people. He did not have much sympathy for anyone he thought was lazy, and if he thought you had potential and didn't realize it—that you *could* have done something if you had worked a little harder—then he didn't have any patience at all.

He was a believer in the work ethic. My mother's side of the family has some of that too. We are impatient with ourselves if we don't do our best, and we feel impatient with waste: Don't waste your time. Don't waste your mind. Don't waste your energy. Don't *waste*.

My grandmother was Mary Finney Muse, who was half African American and half American Indian and had long, beautiful black hair. On the farm, the big meal was at noon—and I can still remember her killing the chicken for it. I tried that once, but I don't think I did it very well. The menu at her house was always pretty much the same: boiled potatoes and cabbage, which she cooked a little too long. When the crops were ready, they would have a tobacco-pulling party, and my grandmother would cook a big meal for all those who were working to get in the harvest.

Sometimes my grandparents came to visit us, since Penhook was only about twenty-five miles from Danville. My parents never knew when they were coming; on Sunday afternoon they would just show up, and we would be so glad to see them. Today, you call and say, "You going to be home?" but it was different back then. You would just stop by. And of course, the doors were unlocked, so if someone wasn't home, you would just go in and wait until they came back. Now I have a key to my house, but when I was growing up, you just came and went, and nobody bothered you.

On the other side of the family, my mother's parents were Charles and Mary Swan Smith, who lived in Almagro, a suburb of Danville. My great-uncle, Moses Smith, had a grocery store there. My grandfather died early on, so I don't have memories of him, but I do remember my grandmother, who was a very economical lady. Whenever there was a church picnic or any church event, Grandma Mary would be the one who would slice the ham for the sandwiches, and she would slice it so thin that you could see through it. She and my grandfather had five children: my mother, Maud; Delilah ("Aunt D"); Zetella; Cecelius ("Uncle C"); and Russell. For most of our younger lives, my grandmother was very active, but it got to the point where she was unable to get around, and finally, as many families did in those days, we had her come live with us.

Frankie's parents, Maude and William B. Muse, Sr., ca. 1950.

My Parents

My father, William Brown Muse—a lot of people called him "Brown"—was a graduate of Pittsylvania Industrial Normal and Collegiate Institute (P.I.N. and C. Institute) at Gretna, Virginia. In 1913, he took the post-office examination and became the third black person in Virginia to be employed as a railroad postal clerk. He was in charge of processing the mail on the train, so he had to travel a great deal between Richmond and Danville, usually three or four days at a time. The postal workers had a union, the National Alliance of Postal Employees, and in 1968, while I was on the U.S. Commission on Civil Rights, I spoke to them at their national convention. My father kept up constantly with legislation to improve things for them.

He was also a historian—he *knew* history—and wanted us to know it too. I think he and my mother bought every book ever written about black history. They taught us the "Negro National Anthem," and we stood at the sound of the very first note. Until he died, my father was a Republican because he admired President Abraham Lincoln, and he liked it that Republicans had opposed expanding slavery before the Civil War and favored civil rights afterward. As adults, we would come back home for visits, and, as we talked politics, he would give us the history of what the Democrats had done in Virginia. What debates we had, family debates! My brothers, sister, and I had become Democrats—by then President Harry S Truman had desegregated the military—but my father still didn't think we were very smart in our choice of parties. He was proud of us though, and he would never have defended the Republicans today with their attacks on equal opportunity and affirmative action.

For a time, he also ran a grocery store on some property he owned just a few blocks from our house, but he told us later he had given up that business before his children ate him out of all the profits. In his off hours, he was a gardener and a baseball fan who enjoyed watching our little local black team play. After his funeral in 1958, we were all sharing memories of my father when I said something I believe even more strongly today: that we didn't appreciate enough how well he had provided for us. Even during the Depression we were blessed, because he was employed by the government and he and our mother managed their resources well.

When Frank Muse got into trouble during those hard years and was about to lose his farm, my father was able to step in and buy it back to save it from foreclosure. And when I went to college, I did not request financial aid; I took for granted my parents would pay the expenses, and they always did.

My mother, Maud Beatrice Smith Muse, was an outgoing person, very involved in the community, and an active sponsor of programs that brought nationally known black speakers and musicians to Danville. Among the speakers were educator Mary McLeod Bethune and Robert S. Abbott, founder and publisher of the *Chicago Defender*; among the musicians were Dorothy Maynor, Marian Anderson, Roland Hayes, and Mahalia Jackson. My mother had a team of black and white female friends who sold tickets to the concerts, which were held in the local armory. Because of segregation, whites sat on one side of the room and blacks on the other; because of segregation in the hotels, many of these visitors stayed with our family or neighbors. When Marian Anderson came to town in the early 1950s, she stayed with the Harraways, two doors down. Her fee for that appearance was $4,500 altogether—a huge amount for that time—with $1,000 as a retainer, and $3,500 paid on the day of the performance. I recall that when my mother went down to the bank to get that cashier's check for $3,500, people along Ross Street came quietly out to stand on their porches and watch her carry that big check down to the Harraways' house.

As a 1911 graduate of Hampton Institute, my mother was also active in Hampton's alumni association and served as its president for fifteen years. Like the rest of my family, she believed that you had to get an education, and, once you had it, nobody could take it away from you. She *knew* that all her children were going to college—the only question was whether it would be Hampton, Virginia State, Virginia Union, Howard, Shaw, or Fisk—and she raised scholarship funds to help others go as well. Before her marriage and for a year afterward, she was a teacher in the Danville Public Schools, then she became a homemaker and taught many things to her own children. Language was important to her, and if you did not spell or pronounce a word properly she would correct you. We could not end a sentence with a preposition, heaven forbid! But she never had to tell me to read; I loved to do it, and I would read anything.

My mother's father, Charles Smith, had been one of the charter members of Calvary Baptist Church in Danville, an all-black church that had been founded in 1892 by a group of forty people—the "Immortal Forty," they called them—who were then only twenty-seven years past the Civil War and slavery. Both my parents were very active at Calvary; my father was a deacon and my mother was a Sunday-school teacher, deaconess, and member of an auxiliary, the Philathea Society. By the time of my first memory of the church, it had grown into one of the largest in Danville, with a membership of some two thousand people.

Calvary, which was located at the corner of Holbrook and Calvary Streets, was within easy walking distance, just four blocks from our home. As children, we went to church, to Sunday school, to *anything* that was happening there. We usually had some part in the program; I often recited poems by Paul Laurence Dunbar or President Lincoln's Gettysburg Address. Of course, we had a strong grounding in the Bible. We read it, we studied it, we memorized it. Like my mother, I also loved singing spirituals; her favorite, I remember, was "It Is Well with My Soul." For us, church attendance was never debatable. It didn't matter if an event was in the afternoon or the evening; we were there. At times we thought there was something else we could be doing, but we were *still* there. We were *involved*, in other words.

We all knew we had our parents' love but we also wanted to earn their respect, because they were disappointed if we didn't do what we should. They were strict. In our younger years, they would talk to us if we did something bad, and if it was really out of sight, we got a whipping. But that was only in the early years; my parents didn't have any stupid children, and after a while we learned. We could still get in trouble, though. I remember one time when I was in high school: It was a beautiful afternoon and three or four of us decided to skip class and walk over to a friend's house on Main Street. We stayed there talking, longer than we meant to, probably more than two hours. When I finally got home, did I catch it! I never, ever in life thought I would stay out of school again. It was as if I had *quit* school. Another time, my brother Tweed was out front, playing ball in the street, as children did. My mother went to the door and said, "Dinner is ready." Tweed kept playing and said, "Later." Well, my mother just stood there and looked at him as if he had lost his mind, and then he saw her and said, "*Uh-oh.*" He put his ball right down and went in.

My parents were protective too. For safety's sake, my father would take us places. And if we brought someone home, we had to expect questions: "Who are they? Who is their father, their mother?" So they were watchful of us.

They also believed that character is built by self-discipline. If you said you were going to do something, you should do it. If someone asked, "When are you going to do this?" and you replied, "I'm fixing to do it," he or she would say, "You're not *fixing* to do it, just *do* it." That is still the same now. If you are asked to do something and you say you are going to do it, then get going. Do it.

Today, people's attitudes toward discipline have changed, but I know that my parents had the same attitude their parents did. They thought that strong discipline was helpful. I remember one time a few years ago when someone brought a child to my house and he began jumping up and down on the sofa. I looked to the mother to stop him but she said, "He is just expressing himself." Well, I wanted the child to stop, and I had a hard time keeping from expressing *myself* to tell her that she ought to do something about it.

My Neighborhood

We lived right next door to the pastor of our church, Reverend George Washington Goode, whose ministry began in 1896 and lasted until 1952—fifty-six years in all. He was a visionary in terms of young people and their needs; he had a youth department, with all kinds of programs and activities. He was also an outstanding community leader, who established the local black hospital and served as its first president. He had founded the school my father attended, P.I.N. and C. Institute, because there were no secondary schools for black students in the county.

But living next door to him was difficult. We always had to be especially good because if we weren't, then Reverend Goode would preach about it. One time he called our house and asked to speak to my father.

He said, "I would like to speak to Mr. Muse. Is he there?" I replied, "No, he is not"—but I did not say "sir." The next Sunday, in his sermon, he began talking about young people and how they "didn't understand about being polite any more." Although he didn't mention my name, I was just sliding down in my seat; I knew he was talking to me.

Our family was lucky. We were comfortably situated in a nice residential area; you might say that we were members of the "black bourgeoisie," but people in Danville just would have called us "well off." To the other side, our neighbor was the bank president, and the undertaker was across the street. We had a phone in our front hallway, though not everyone did; the Harraways did not have one, so people would call us whenever they wanted to speak to Mrs. Harraway. A couple of times a day, one of us children would have to run down to get her to come answer the phone—and we got a little tired of it. The Harraways had a car, though, and we did not.

Our house had a big porch in the front and a large yard out back where my father had his garden. Inside were nine rooms, including four bedrooms; we were lucky enough to have indoor plumbing. On the first floor, there was a living room, dining room, and my father's office, where, as postal clerk, he kept cards for each train stop between Richmond and Danville. Like her own mother, my mother spent a lot of time in the kitchen since she loved cooking—and I do too. Even now, there is one thing people want to know if I invite them to dinner: am I going to give them corn pudding? My mother made it, as well as the most delicious caramel cake and sweet potato pies. We all loved sweet potatoes, and she would keep a supply on the stove, ready to eat. In those days, doctors made house calls, and when Dr. Winslow came to our house, before he would even check us out, he might go into the kitchen and get a sweet potato to snack on.

On the surrounding blocks were some of our relatives. My mother's first cousin, Jeanette Smith, lived with her family on the 300 block of Ross Street; other cousins lived around the corner on Holbrook. So we primarily socialized with people in the few blocks around us; we went to church nearby, to school, to the shops where we were welcome. We were pretty much within walking distance of everywhere we wanted to go.

Now we speak of being raised by a village, but then we just thought of it as a neighborhood. You might be out front roller-skating or playing ball, but your parents did not have to watch you as long as there was anybody on a front porch. If Mrs. Harraway caught us misbehaving, for example, she did not hold back. She would say something like, "What is the matter with you?" You also had to be well groomed and dress properly; you had to look your best. Someone was always saying to one of my brothers: "Child, your shirttail is out!" There are times now when I see a boy whose shirttail is out, and I want to say: "Put your shirttail in!" When I was growing up, nobody would have hesitated to tell me that my slip was showing. That is something I remember Mary McLeod Bethune saying a long time ago. "If my slip is showing, *tell* me. I'm the only one who can do anything about it." When people told us things then, it had a value we didn't appreciate, but I do appreciate it now. Whenever they said, "Don't do this," "Watch your step," or "Wash your hands," it was a sign of friendship and love.

Since a lot of our living was done close to home, traveling anywhere was special, a real treat. My brother Andy likes to tell the story about the time I was going to a young people's convention in Dryfork, Virginia, and I had to take the train. I was so proud of that! My father took me to the station and I decided that I had better have a magazine for my long trip. Now the first problem was that the magazine I chose happened to be a "true confessions" kind of magazine, which did not please my father one bit. But he also told me that by the time I got it open, I would be where I was going. Dryfork, which seemed like such a long, important journey to me, was really only nine miles away.

My Brothers and Sisters

I am the oldest of eight children, six of whom grew to adulthood. I was born first, on November 24, 1916. Next came my brother "Bill"—William B. Muse, Jr.—who is two years younger than I am. He graduated from Hampton in 1940 and was president and CEO of the Imperial Savings and Loan Association in Martinsville, Virginia, until his retirement in 1992.

"Tweed" followed: Charles Sumner Muse, a year younger than Bill, who was named for his grandfather and for the abolitionist senator Charles Sumner. He attended Hampton for three years until he was drafted in 1941, then went back to West Virginia State College after his discharge. He received his Ed.D. degree from Oklahoma University in 1966 and taught at South Carolina State College until his death in 1989.

My third brother, Edward, was two years younger than Tweed; at birth his name was Elijah Barnette and he was called "Barnette" as a child, but as an adult he changed his name to Edward B. Muse. He received bachelor's and master's degrees from the New School of Social Work in New York City. From 1964 to 1986, he was director of life membership for the NAACP and remained active in the organization until his death in 1997.

Next came Virginia, who died in infancy, then my sister Maudena, named for my mother. In 1943, she graduated from John M. Langston High School and then spent a year at Shaw before returning home to Danville for the summer. But Maudena became ill and died of pneumonia in September 1944, just as I entered law school.

Following her was my sister Allie, ten years younger than I am, a retired educator who taught at St. Augustine College in Raleigh, North Carolina, and still lives there. Allie, her three children, and her grand-daughter are all Hampton graduates; in fact, Allie recently won an alumni award from Hampton. She has done the same thing my mother did: help people get financial aid so they can attend Hampton.

The youngest in the family is my brother Andy, known as "A. C." while he was growing up, who attended Wilberforce University in Ohio and received his law degree from Lincoln University in Missouri. He practiced law in Danville for twelve years, then later worked as a staff member for the national Democratic Party. Now he lives in Williamsburg, Virginia, and is counsel to the president of Raytheon International, an aircraft company.

We often did things as a family: eating all our meals, praying, preparing for Sunday school, playing games together. Each of us had to learn some musical instrument—we could have had our own orchestra. Bill played the clarinet, Tweed and Barnette learned the trombone and sang, and I played piano. Of course, that meant when the pianist was not present at church, I would fill in. Until a few years ago, I still did that in my current church's Sunday school.

The Muse family in Danville, Virginia, 1954. Left to right: front row—Frankie, William Muse (father), Maude Muse (mother), and Allie (sister); back row—William, Charles, Edward, and Andrew (brothers).

Continuing Family Ties

In June 1954, my mother was ill, but she got better and wrote to us, asking us to come home in August. We all managed to be there, and she arranged for a photographer to stop by that Sunday. However, he was late in arriving, and my brother Bill, who had come prepared to play golf, said that he didn't want to wait any longer. I said, "Bill, you stay so that we can take this picture. This might be the last time we are all together." I will never forget saying that. Bill did stay, and the picture was taken; then on October 29, I got a call: "Frankie, your mother is gone." I said, "Gone *where?*" We had thought she was fine, but she had died suddenly.

After her death, my family got together regularly for funerals and weddings, and in 1974, I organized the first Muse family reunion, which was held in St. Louis. At that event, my brother Andy brought each of his brothers and sisters a ring he'd had made to symbolize the binding together in our family. A diamond in the ring represented our parents' teaching to "Let your light shine." That was his gift to us, and then we got together and had the jeweler make one for him too.

Since then, we have had an annual Muse family reunion, held in different locations, but we have changed the name to "Muse-Smith" to include the maternal side as well. In 2000, we held our reunion in Danville. On the first day, we had a seminar on investments and financial planning; at each reunion we have some sort of educational program. This time, Andy also sponsored a big party at the renovated train station, with more than one hundred people in attendance. As a family, we worshiped at Calvary that Sunday. It was wonderful to see Danville again. Ross Street is still Ross Street, but the big frame house we lived in has been torn down, and the person who bought the property built a new brick house on the site. My family gave Calvary the property my father once owned, where his grocery store was located, and they have used it for a parking lot. What used to be our neighborhood has changed, but we certainly did enjoy living there.

The Muse-Smith family reunion in St. Louis, 1983.

Responding to Prejudice

My parents felt that, if you stand for something, there are times when you have to say, "Enough." Taking a stand may not mean that you scream and carry on; rather, you try to do something that will be effective.

When we were children, for instance, the public-transit system in Danville was segregated. So, instead of riding on the streetcar and sitting at the back, we simply walked everywhere. We could have gotten on that streetcar and said, "Now I will take a stand" and been arrested, but there are different ways to take a stand. There are also times when you are limited in your choices. When I went to Hampton from Danville by train—a journey of several hundred miles—I did not have a choice, and I rode in the back. Sometimes when you beat your head against a brick wall, you have to realize that you are damaging your head, not hurting the wall. Therefore, you do the best you can so long as you do not acquiesce and you do not give up. You say, "Later for *you*," and promise yourself that when you *can* do something about it, you will.

In Danville, everything was segregated, including the churches. The nearest black movie theater was in Greensboro, North Carolina—forty-eight miles away. If we wanted to go to one of the segregated theaters in Danville, we would have to sit at the top of the balcony. Friends sometimes tried to shop at a local department store, and if they found a piece of clothing they liked, they were not allowed to try it on. If my mother heard of something like that, there was no *way* that we would ever go there.

But we didn't buy a whole lot of clothes from stores anyway. In those days, you had things made by black dressmakers in town or you made them yourself. I remember once that my teacher at school, a stylish young woman, had a new outfit, a velvet coat with a fur collar. I have always loved beautiful clothes, and I thought that coat was just gorgeous. So I took the design to our tailor and had him copy it as my new "Sunday-go-to-meeting" coat. When my teacher saw me in that coat, at some program in school, she just had a fit—it was a compliment, but not one that she appreciated.

The library was segregated too—you did not go to the big library; the black community had its own. That is also how we got our own bank, the First State Bank, which was started in 1915 by black people who wanted to borrow money from a white-owned bank and could not. Relatives of mine were among that group, and so was Reverend Goode; in fact, he served as its chairman for many years. Today it is still black owned, and by now it probably has more white depositors than black. It also has a new building, just finished recently, and it is beautiful. From the beginning, my family held stock in that bank; I do too, and I always will.

My parents did not feel any hostility toward white people, just toward ignorance and prejudice. I must say that many of the things I would later fight as a member of the U.S. Commission on Civil Rights—hatred and violence—I never actually encountered as a child. I'm not saying that they didn't happen in Danville, but I never encountered them. There were things that *did* happen, though. Under court order, Danville had to desegregate its library—so it just took out all of its chairs. Well, how ridiculous did that make them look! You can imagine all of the cartoons that were printed about Danville. Then quietly, without saying anything, they put the chairs back.

Even as a child, I always had a very low tolerance for things like this, and my parents knew it. I was like my grandfather in that respect—I didn't "take no stuff" either. I think they were nervous about my reaction to the segregated streetcars, and what might happen if I got on one and decided to take a stand. What made me this way? I don't know, except that I knew from an early age that the Constitution said we were all "created equal," and that means we *are* equal. When it comes to segregation, to prejudice, I just won't take it.

By the early 1950s, there had been many changes. My mother was on the board of the YWCA and had been active in the community alongside white people, including some from our neighboring block. I remember that, after her death, I flew right away to Danville, and by that evening my brothers and sister had arrived too. As I walked into our dining room, I saw that it was full of food. I asked my brother who had brought it, and he told me: it had come from our white neighbors on the 100 block of Ross Street.

We appreciated this thoughtfulness, but an incident en route to Danville had also reminded me that there was still much work to be done. I had had to change planes in Louisville, Kentucky, and during my layover, I went into the airport coffee shop and sat down, waiting to be served.

The waitress came over, said "I can't serve you," and asked me to leave. But I didn't leave; I knew my mother would not want me to get up. I told the waitress she *had* to serve me.

Instead, she called the police. When the officer arrived, I told him I was a lawyer, on my way to my mother's funeral, and it was illegal for them not to serve me. I said, "Arrest me if you want to." He did not, but the waitress told all the other customers they had to leave and then closed the restaurant. I went outside and called an NAACP attorney in Louisville, James Crumlin, and told him what had happened. Although I had to go on to Danville, he said he would file a complaint against the coffee shop. A few weeks later, I learned that it had been desegregated.

My Early Education

Separate schools for blacks and whites were a way of life. We all attended the "Negro school" and lived and thought in the context of black education. In Danville, the black community was assertive, so our school was probably better than most. Yet we did not have all the resources that the white school did—and my brothers, sister, and I talked often about how much we missed. Occasionally, there were also "incidents." One time the choir went on a visit somewhere to sing at a concert and they were not allowed to be visible. I wasn't along on that trip, and it was just as well because I certainly would have walked out.

One of the teachers I remember well was "Miss Kate"—Mrs. Mary Kate Taylor Page—a dear friend of my family. My first name, Marie, came from hers. Miss Kate taught me in sixth grade and then kept up with me; she demanded a lot of me, but she also encouraged me. That was a hallmark of all the teachers. On the other hand, if you were not a good student, your mother would know before you ever got home. She did not need a report card.

In November 1953, Miss Kate invited me to come back as the guest speaker for the Women's Day celebration at Calvary. I still have the letter she sent me: "My dear Frankie," she wrote. "At long last it seems that one of my cherished dreams is about to be realized...to say that I am happy is putting it mildly—all I can say is that God answers prayer." It was a wonderful experience for me, and my parents were very proud. I have a letter from my mother, written in December of that year, that says, "Daddy has not finished swelling over you yet."

As I look back on it now, I think that the black community in Danville was unusually committed to education. A larger-than-average percentage of black high-school graduates went on to college from Danville. All over the community, people like my mother were working to make sure students did not miss out on a college education just because they did not have the money. The churches contributed, sororities contributed, individuals helped out. Just so long as that student was good enough to go, and wanted to go, the community was committed to making it possible for him or her to do that. I never, ever heard of a student from Danville, who had the ability and the interest, being denied a college education because of inadequate resources.

For instance, there was Camilla Williams, a Danville native who went on to become an internationally known opera star and faculty member at Indiana University. She was a member of Calvary, and I used to accompany her on the piano when she sang. Her parents were not college trained themselves, but she had a wonderful soprano voice and everyone knew that, so when Camilla went to Virginia State, people from Danville helped her in whatever way they could. In the mid-1950s, Camilla Williams came home from Vienna and sang in Danville, and I think that three thousand people, white and black, came out to hear her.

When I went on to Westmoreland High School (now John M. Langston High School), I was an A student—except in algebra. Mr. Gibson, the principal, told me, "You did not make it in algebra and I am not going to pass you." That was devastating. How in the world could that happen? For some reason, "x plus whatever" didn't get through to me the first time, so I had to take that course again. When I did, my father helped me get through it.

So I made it, and I was valedictorian of my high-school class in 1933. I received a couple of awards, including a $50 award from the Alpha Kappa Alpha sorority, in which my mother was a patron mother. At my graduation, we had baccalaureate services, and the girls all wore dresses we had made in home-economics class. I'm sure my parents were proud of me, but I don't particularly remember that: I think they had expected nothing less. In their view, and mine, I had just done what I was supposed to do.

Chapter Two

Doing My Homework
From Hampton to Howard

1933–47

AT AGE SIXTEEN, I GRADUATED from high school and went off by train—my longest train ride ever—to Hampton Institute, a beautiful school right on the water in the Tidewater area of southeastern Virginia. The college had been founded in 1868 to educate emancipated slaves, and even today the Emancipation Oak, where Abraham Lincoln was said to have given the first southern reading of the Emancipation Proclamation, is an important campus landmark.

I had left Danville, a rather sheltered community, but I found that Hampton was also sheltered in a different kind of way. For instance, you had to have the written consent of your parents before you could go to town, and, if you did go, you went in a group. Even then, you only went shopping, and only to a place where you could get what you wanted without any hassle. You would never, *ever* spend your money where they didn't want it. If I was in a store and a white person came up behind me and the clerk helped that person first, I would leave—and I still do.

At Hampton, I lived in Virginia Hall, now Virginia Cleveland Hall, a lovely old dormitory. My roommate, Minnie Moore, had a beautiful alto voice that my classmates and I loved to listen to when we got together after dinner. We also had a matron in the dorm, who would check our rooms regularly to make sure they were clean. Time and time again, she would tell us that Booker T. Washington, who had graduated from Hampton in 1876, kept his room so clean you could eat off the floor. We got a little tired of hearing about Booker T. Washington!

While the matron was checking on our rooms, she would check on us too. I remember that when I had my first menstrual period at college, I had cramps, so I stayed in bed as usual. The matron came in and said, "Why are you still in bed?" I told her I had cramps, and she said again, "Why are you still in bed? You either go to the infirmary and get something for it or you go to class." I thought that was cruel, but I went, and that was the last time I ever stayed in bed.

I chose to major in mathematics, and, as one of my electives, I took typing; later on, in my law office, I was awfully glad I had. I was a good student but not an outstanding one. What I enjoyed most was having pretty clothes, going to dances and parties, and being popular. I was elected president of the Phyllis Wheatley Club, a social club for female students; I was also a charter member of the Hampton Dance Club, which was devoted to modern dance.

At times I did question the rules. For instance, there was nowhere to go to get your hair straightened, which was something that everyone did in those days—it was part of your routine grooming. So I organized a group, and they found a place for us, in the room where we did our hand laundry. Once in while, I would also do things that I had never dared to try before. In my sophomore year, a group of us wanted to see what it was like to smoke cigarettes. I said to them, "You know it *is* against the rules, and if they catch us, we are going to be disciplined." We thought about it for a while—and decided to put a wet towel over the transom so nobody could smell the smoke!

I was a little homesick, but I had relatives nearby who would sometimes pick me up and take me places. My brother Bill also became a student while I was there, though I didn't see him too much. And I did go home for Christmas and the summer holiday, and in between my family sent me care packages with food inside.

By June 1936, when I had been at Hampton for three years, I knew that I wanted to be a lawyer. Racial segregation and discrimination were pervasive, and I was always saying to myself, "Later for *you*." I wanted to change things, to do *something* that would be effective. So I left Hampton a year early and went to New York City, intending to live with my mother's sister, Aunt D, and go to law school; somehow I heard of St. John's University and decided that was where I would matriculate. But when I got there, St. John's informed me that they did not recognize Hampton's credits—I had never dreamed that some universities did not recognize credits from black colleges. What a detour! But I decided to stay in New York and take courses in bookkeeping so that I could qualify for an office job, while I figured out what to do next with my life.

New York City in the 1930s

I moved in with Aunt D, who had an extra bedroom in her brownstone on 130th Street and Lenox Avenue in Harlem, and she became a surrogate mother to me. At that time she was separated from her husband, Roy, who was in real estate; she lived with her son, Buster, a musician who was also appointed to a job in the post office, and her daughter, Marjorie, who was disabled. And I was in *New York*—the place you wanted to go, if you were living in the South. New York drew people; everything great was supposed to be happening there. Sometimes people would get there and wonder, "Is *this* all there is?" I remember thinking that everyone in New York would have a mansion, but they had ordinary homes. I loved it anyway.

Right away, though, I had a lot of adjustments to make. People I met sometimes laughed at me a little for my southern accent or expressions, like when I would say "yonder," "listen y'all," or "What y'all talking about?" Suddenly, I also had to get used to a much faster paced, and much less polite, way of life. How could I ever learn to push my way onto a crowded bus or subway car? And how could I pass people on the street without saying hello? I quickly found out that New Yorkers think the United States map is New York, and the rest of the country is overseas somewhere.

I discovered something else surprising: that those of us who went north were expecting too much in the way of integration. We thought everything would be "peaches and cream," that everybody would be welcoming—and they were not. On the other hand, I could get on the subway in New York like anyone else if I had five cents for a ride, and for fifteen cents I could go to any movie I wanted.

So there I was, living in Harlem, which was known at that time as the "Negro Capital of America." Famous jazz musicians such as Ella Fitzgerald and Chick Webb were performing there in those years. If you heard that Coleman Hawkins or Louis Armstrong was appearing, you would just have to be there. I went to the Apollo Theatre for concerts, and in those days, I think it cost twenty-five cents. Since Buster played guitar in a little combo on weekends, I got to hear some music through him too. I loved going dancing at Small's Paradise and the Savoy Ballroom, two of the most popular places in Harlem.

Aunt D was very much like my mother, outgoing and assertive. As a member of Abyssinian Baptist Church, she was a longtime friend of Adam Clayton Powell, Sr., who was from Franklin County, Virginia, and had been senior minister at Abyssinian for more than twenty years. In 1937, Adam Clayton Powell, Jr., also a minister, took over from his father and became pastor of Abyssinian. He began a campaign against white-owned Harlem businesses that would not hire blacks. Politics also interested him; in 1941, he was elected to the New York City Council, then three years later to the U.S. Congress.

I knew I wanted to join some church; at home I had grown up in Calvary—it had been my support group and part of my being. And in those days, the perception was that Abyssinian was *the* church in Harlem. So I joined an active young people's group there led by Maxine Dargan, who became a dear friend. Adam, who was aggressively opposed to discrimination, worked closely with the group and helped teach us the basics of government: what its responsibilities were, how to get involved, how to get to know people, and how to let them know who *you* are. The group became a kind of training ground for political action and community involvement, and I felt inspired by the fact that we were really going to make a difference. Adam was also an eloquent speaker—charismatic, visionary—and I admired him very much.

One time, we traveled by bus to Pittsburgh for a conference, and the young women in our group—which was mixed, black and white—were supposed to stay at the YWCA, but when we got there, they would not take us. So we all sat on the steps, as a group, until they found somewhere else for us to stay. While I would not have been at all surprised if that kind of thing had happened in the South, I was shocked that it had happened in Pittsburgh. That was a learning experience for me, when I thought such things were behind me.

In the youth group, I met a young man named Shelby Freeman from St. Louis. He had graduated with a major in mathematics from a good school, but one that I, as a southerner who knew little about the Midwest, had not yet heard of: Lincoln University in Jefferson City, Missouri. When he wanted to go on to graduate school, the University of Missouri was not accepting black students, but they would pay for him to go outside the state, so he came to Columbia Teacher's College in New York on a State of Missouri Fellowship. I thought Shelby was handsome and very personable. We hit it off right away and started dating. On our first date, as I recall, I went out with Shelby and a friend of his—but I liked Shelby better because of his beautiful dimples. Much later, I asked him how he felt about me that night, and he said he thought I was "cute."

During our courtship, we went to movies, did some dancing—things that we could afford. It was still the Depression, after all, and nobody had much money. At the time, Shelby was living in a small room in Harlem somewhere, but I never even saw it. I could not go there with him—no way!

Shelby and Frankie, late 1940's.

Then, on December 15, 1938—to the distress of my parents and his, who had not even met one another—we quietly got married in the Chapel of Divine Compassion, an Episcopal church in New York.

Apartments were scarce in those days, so at first we lived with another couple and their two children at 217 West 110th Street, across from Central Park. In August 1939, our daughter, Shelbe Patricia "Pat," was born, and we moved in for a while with Aunt D while Shelby took a teaching job with the Works Progress Administration (WPA). Finally, we got an apartment of our own at 135th Street and Lenox Avenue, and that is where we were in March 1941 when Shelby was offered a civil-service job with the Department of the Army in Washington, D.C.

Jennie Freeman (mother-in-law), Shelby holding daughter Pat, and Frankie, ca. 1940.

Washington in the War Years

In Washington, we found our first apartment on P Street Northwest. The city was a hectic, exciting place during the war years, with crowds of outsiders flooding in. Everybody was working—if you could do *anything*, you were working, and otherwise you were in the military. Because of his weak eyes, my husband was not drafted, but my brothers were. Bill was able to graduate from Hampton first, but Tweed had only finished three years, so he decided to start over again at college when he got out.

With my daughter, Pat, in day care, I got a job as a clerk with the Department of the Treasury in Foreign Funds Control, while also taking courses in statistics through a graduate program sponsored by the Department of Agriculture. All this time, Shelby and I tried to organize our schedules so we could be present for Pat's school programs. By 1943, when I had not yet received a promotion, I applied for transfer to the Office of Price Administration (OPA). As I left, my supervisor in Foreign Funds Control told me she was sorry I was transferring because otherwise she would have promoted me.

Frankie's daughter, Pat, 1940.   *Pat, ca. 1958.*

Frankie with daughter, Pat, ca. 1942.

I am not so sure that would have happened, however. I had been one of the first black employees in the department, and at holiday time one of the white employees had brought some dolls to work to sell—she called them "Mammy dolls." I took offense and complained, and everyone thought I was being hypersensitive. Just at that point I completed a project that was marked outstanding, but on my evaluation my performance was only rated as satisfactory, and I felt that this was a result of my complaint. I did not confront anyone about this, but I quietly decided to leave.

There were occasional things that happened outside of work too. For a time, Shelby, Pat, and I lived in Arlington, Virginia, where the buses were segregated. Most times the drivers didn't enforce the rule, so I could get on in Washington and sit wherever I wanted on the ride home. But one time I got on the bus in Washington and sat down in the front, then when we got to Virginia the driver made me move to the back. That time I did move, reluctantly; this kind of thing happened from time to time to all of us in those days. I just put it aside, and said to myself: "Later for *you.*"

The OPA was a better job—a higher, professional-level grade—and I was more comfortable with my coworkers. A few months later, I ran into Martin A. Martin, a Danville lawyer who had become a Justice Department attorney; his brother, Conrad Martin, was the president of First State Bank. The Martin family had been friends of ours while I was growing up, and I regarded Martin, who was a successful lawyer and a few years older than I was, as a role model. Now he challenged me, saying: "What happened to *you*?" I told him I was planning to go to law school—and he replied "When?" He wanted to pin me down. "Howard is right here," he added. There were other law schools, too, but Howard University School of Law *was* there, and it was the mecca.

Starting out at Howard

After that conversation I decided to act, so in June 1944 I took a day off work and went to see Dean William H. Hastie of the Howard University School of Law, which was located on the Howard campus in the basement of Founder's Library. I told him I was very aware of

Shelby, Frankie, and Pat, 1948.

Howard's history and wanted to find out how to get into law school. He said: "Mrs. Freeman, have you *applied?*" I felt so stupid because here I was, sitting in the dean's office, and I had not done the first thing you should do, which is file the application.

That night, I told Shelby that I had decided I wanted to go to law school. Shelby said, "Do you? Well, all right." Then I said the dean had also told me that students could not work if they went to law school— and at that point Shelby really had to do some thinking, because of the tuition and the expenses, but he still said, "OK." I called my parents to see whether they could help us; they had been disappointed that I had not gone to law school before, and I knew that they would do whatever they could for us. Shelby's parents offered to help too. We also knew that Pat was in a good day-care center and would soon begin elementary school.

So that September I started law school, but I decided to try working at least part-time at the OPA. That lasted about two months. I just couldn't do it, and Shelby could see how it was, even when he did as much as he could. But with the support we got from our families, we could make it without my income—and that support made me more determined than ever that I would not waste any time.

Today, I have a picture on my wall by African American artist Charles White, which shows a tired student bent over her books. I think of that picture as *me*. Because I did not want to interfere with our family time, I would get up at 3 A.M. to study when my husband and daughter were asleep. All the while, I was very aware that I was not only a student but also a wife and mother; for example, I considered it my responsibility to prepare breakfast and dinner for my family each and every day. There were times when I prayed daily, even hourly, "Lord, let me get through this day." Of course, Shelby was a great help, and together we somehow managed to make it. I did not think my classmates knew what I was going through because most of them were men, but afterward some of them told me that the support I got was incredible.

Since it was wartime, we did not have a large class—there were only about thirty of us. I think we all felt that first year was a revelation. We had to learn to do a different kind of studying, to keep our minds focused on the issues and avoid irrelevancies. As Dean Hastie, who taught

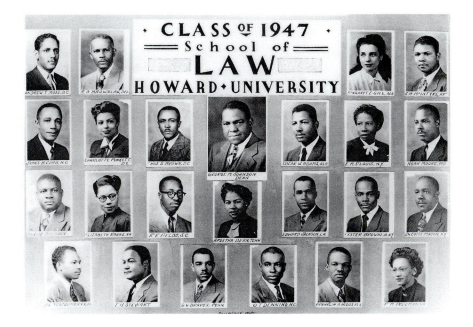

Howard University law school class of 1947. Frankie is in lower right corner.

us evidence, would say: "Talk like a lawyer." In other words, begin with the facts, find out what the issue is, and stay on the track. If we did not, he would tell us, point blank: "That was irrelevant." I took in all that he said, and today I find that I do those things instinctively. Somebody will call and say, "I want you to do something," and I'll say, "Now wait a minute. First of all, tell me *exactly* what you are talking about."

Many of Howard's faculty members at that time were giants in their field—all excellent at what they did but different in personality. Dean Hastie, who served as dean from 1939 to 1946, was a Harvard graduate and later chief judge of the U.S. Court of Appeals for the Third Circuit in Philadelphia; in 1946, while I was a student, he was appointed governor of the Virgin Islands, the first African American to serve in that position. He was scholarly, professorial, very thorough in the training he gave us.

My torts professor, Spottswood Robinson, was younger than Dean Hastie and more informal in his style but as sharp as could be. We remained friends after law school; much later, he was my predecessor on the U.S. Commission on Civil Rights and then was named a federal judge. Along with Oliver Hill and Martin A. Martin, who became his law partners in Richmond, Virginia, he was also part of a team that fought many important civil rights battles.

Another eminent faculty member from Howard's recent past was Charles H. Houston, a Harvard law graduate who had been a faculty member at Howard, then dean of the law school from 1930 to 1935. By the time I was a student, he had become the first chief legal counsel for the NAACP, and I met him through my work with the NAACP a little later. Charles Houston was a mentor to Thurgood Marshall and pioneered the 1954 *Brown v. Board of Education* decision by the U.S. Supreme Court that outlawed segregation in the public schools. In 1958, Howard's law school renamed its main building after Charles Houston.

My fellow students also included some people who developed strong legal reputations. A dear friend, Juanita Kidd Stout, was my classmate for one year while she also worked part-time as secretary to Charles Houston; as an undergraduate, she had attended Lincoln University with Shelby. After leaving Howard, she went on to finish her J.D. and LL.M. degrees from Indiana University and to clerk for William Hastie when he was sitting on the Third Circuit. Later, she became a distinguished jurist as Judge of the Court of Common Pleas in Philadelphia.

There were others as well. Richard E. Fields became a well-known trial attorney and circuit-court judge in South Carolina. James Cobb went into private practice in Washington, D.C. Oscar Adams became an associate justice of the Alabama Supreme Court, the first black appellate judge in Alabama. George Draper was an assistant circuit attorney in St. Louis, and later a judge in the District of Columbia; his son, George Draper, Jr., became a member of the Missouri Court of Appeals.

Because it was wartime, we had a large number of women in the class—probably six out of the total; today, of course, women would make up half the class. One of my classmates was Charlotte Pinkett Lewis, who took a position with the Equal Employment Opportunity Commission. Viva Young, who was in my study group, went into private practice in Chicago. At that time, only a few women were involved in litigation, and that remained true for many years.

Thurgood Marshall had graduated from Howard in 1933, and he became one of our role models. I first got to know him when he came with his team to Howard to practice his oral arguments on a small group of us while he was preparing to argue several cases before the U.S. Supreme Court. A little later, Thurgood—by then counsel for the NAACP Legal Defense Fund—offered me a job in Baltimore working for the fund, but I could not take it because I was about to move to St. Louis. I admired him so very much: He was an effective civil rights lawyer, and I liked that he worked hard but also enjoyed life. The very experience of listening to him and his team at Howard sharpened my decision to become a civil rights lawyer myself, and I began to pursue that interest in my coursework. In addition to my regular class schedule, I found time to participate in seminars on constitutional law, the Fourteenth Amendment, and legal stratagems to attack racial segregation and discrimination.

Endings and Beginnings

During my second year of law school, I became pregnant—and I was due to deliver in September, just as my third year of law school was about to begin. I wrote to the new dean, George Johnson, and asked whether I could register late for my senior year. He said he could not permit late registration and that I should talk to the registrar, Dean Wilkinson, about my situation.

So on September 10, I went to the registrar and requested permission to register late. He looked at me—I was nine months pregnant—and said, "Mrs. Freeman, I think you should stay out a year and then come back." But Shelby and I could not afford to add an extra year to the process, and I think I was also afraid that if I left school I would never go back. We had also planned that once I graduated we would move to St. Louis, Shelby's hometown; his parents were there, and he was an only child.

So I walked out of the registrar's office and back to the law school, where I got in line with my classmates to register. Those in front of me immediately got *out* of line and let me register for my courses first. Somebody in the dean's office must have told him about this because as soon as I was finished, Miss Cooper, his assistant, came out and said,

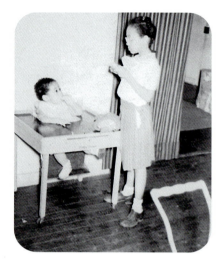

Pat with Butch, 1947.

Shelby and Butch, 1948.

"Dean Johnson wants to see you." So I went to his office and he said, "Now that you are registered, Mrs. Freeman, you can go home and come back after your baby is born and the doctor releases you." So I called Shelby to pick me up, and our son, Shelby Freeman III—"Butch," as we called him—was born four days later.

Two weeks later, the doctor released me and I went back to school while a relative came to stay with us and take care of the baby. Then suddenly, Shelby's plans changed because he was offered a job teaching finance at the Associated Colleges of Upper New York (now the College Center of the Finger Lakes) in upstate New York. With the end of the war, returning veterans needed places to study, and New York State had established a junior-college system to accommodate them. At the same time, reductions were taking place among the civilian employees in the Army, so it was a good time for Shelby to leave. He accepted the job and went to live in Sampson, New York, about thirty-five miles from Ithaca, coming back every other weekend and on holidays.

What a hard, trying year that was, but we made it because of friends and family. A small group of my classmates would come over to study, and, when I was not in class, they would share their notes with me. While many people believed that women belonged at home and not in a male-dominated profession, I did not find that attitude at Howard, which had been open to females from the beginning. In my senior year, one of my professors, who was white, told me, "I wish I could recommend you to Harvard for graduate study, but Harvard doesn't accept women." At that time, Harvard would accept blacks, but not women.

In May 1947, I graduated second in my class to B. A. Brownlow, who was number one. At commencement, one of the faculty members came up to remind me of the day that I stood in line to register and said, "You looked as if you were going to give birth—and as if you wished you could do just that to get back at us!" My mother and my mother-in-law—"Mama Jennie"—both came for the commencement ceremony, which was held on a Saturday. Since my sister, Allie, was graduating from Hampton that Sunday, my mother had to hurry to the train to get there in time. I remember her telling me, "Your daddy is proud, so proud."

As her graduation gift to me, Aunt D stayed in Washington for the weekend to take care of the children so that I could go up to Sampson for a few days. It was a big weekend there; Duke Ellington's band was playing. That was a wonderful break for me, because at that point I was just about *gone*.

Afterward, I came back to Washington to take the District of Columbia bar exam in June, then the children and I joined Shelby at Sampson, where we were planning to live for the year. That August, we made a quick trip to Danville so I could be matron of honor at my sister's wedding. We had gone down a few days early because this was my first visit home since my sister Maudena's death in September 1944. On August 11, we all went to visit my grandmother Mary on the farm. It was hot, and Butch was fretful, but I just thought he was tired.

The next afternoon, a relative saw in the Washington newspapers that I had passed the bar. One of my male classmates kidded me: "Frankie, the only reason you passed was because they thought you were a man." Actually, among the five or six of us who had taken the D.C. bar exam, only two women—Charlotte Pinkett Lewis and I—had passed. That meant I would not only be sworn in as a member of the District of Columbia bar but I could also admitted to the U.S. Court of Appeals.

While that was a wonderful feeling, my euphoria lasted for only a few hours because that night Butch, who was only ten months old, was stricken with a very high fever and convulsions. We rushed him to the hospital, and the pediatrician who treated him thought it was pneumonia; later we discovered that it was actually viral encephalitis. Butch stayed in the hospital for a few days, but soon he was up and about, though he still needed to wear a brace on his leg. We thought he was recovering. We had no idea what would happen later.

A Valuable Experience

I am grateful now for my education at Hampton and at Howard; in fact, I have served as a member of the board of trustees of Howard since 1976, and in 1992 I was elected trustee emeritae. From both institutions I learned so many lessons that I have used in the practice of law. For example, decorum—how you dress and conduct yourself—is important.

If a trial starts at 10 A.M., be at the counsel table with your files open and ready no later than fifteen minutes before that. And don't lose your temper. Have a sense of humor, and see what you can do to move ahead. Try to build on whatever you can.

Most important: Do your homework. The fact that someone does not like you or think much of you because you are black doesn't matter. Do your *homework*. The first jury trial verdict I ever won, against a packing company in St. Louis, was because the opposing lawyer underestimated me. I don't know whether it was because of gender or race or both, but he did not know until the jury was being impaneled that he had a problem—and by then it was too late.

Frankie and other recipients of the Outstanding Alumni Award at the Howard University Charter Day celebration, 1975.

Frankie (second row, fourth from right) at the fifty-year reunion of the Hampton Institute class of 1937, May 1987.

Like other historically black colleges, both Howard and Hampton have given vitality and meaning to the U.S. Constitution and to the statement in the Declaration of Independence that "all men are created equal." They are the only group of educational institutions in this country that have never denied admission to any student because of race, creed, color, or gender. We must recognize that we owe these institutions a debt and rededicate ourselves to their continued survival. As the product of two historically black institutions, I acknowledge that I also have dues that I must pay, and I have tried—and will continue to try—to pay those dues as long as I live.

Chapter Three

"I Am a Lawyer"
Settling in St. Louis
1947–51

UPSTATE NEW YORK IS PRETTY COUNTRY, and we lived near Seneca Lake, the most beautiful lake I have ever seen. That school year, 1947–48, was a complete change for us. For one thing, the junior college was located in Sampson, a small town—very different in size from New York City and Washington, D.C. The weather was so different too. I remember the first snow, the sleds, the heavy clothing. One time we were snowed in for three days, and after you got over the shock, it was quite nice.

Sampson was a busy academic community, full of transplants from many places. As a former military base, it had lots of apartments; all of us lived on campus, and the atmosphere was very cordial. Sar Levitan, the social-policy commentator and economist, and his wife, Brita, were our next-door neighbors and friends. At the time he was writing a book about labor, and he asked me to read his manuscript and comment on parts related to civil rights issues. The Levitans were Jewish, a religion I knew very little about; another Jewish family on campus invited us to share in their Passover Seder—an enriching experience and our first ever.

For a long time, we were the only black faculty family on campus. Because everyone was so friendly to us, it took us a while to realize that we were actually the first black people some of them had ever met. I think some people thought we had beautiful tans because they didn't have any idea who we were. Once I went to a tea for faculty wives, and the other wives asked me more questions than I wanted to be asked about my background. So we loved Sampson, but we missed our black friends and not being able to read the black press.

In addition to Shelby's job teaching finance, the college offered me a position as an instructor in business law. Since the class load was not heavy I was able to handle it, so I taught for that year and spent time with my children. Pat was in elementary school then; with all the other faculty children, she rode the bus to Ovid, five miles away. As a teacher, I was shocked to give my first test and get back such poor spelling from a room full of white students, who had probably gone to much better schools than most black students did. So in that way I learned an important lesson: students are students, and some can't spell regardless of race *or* the quality of their schools.

All in all, the year was a good transition for us from Washington—the war years, the law-school years, and all of that—an opportunity for us to relax and plan for our move to St. Louis, and for me to take the Missouri Bar. We also made new friends—and, for the first time, we did not make any distinction between whites and blacks, Jews and Christians. Of course, there were some people we were not friendly with, but that is true in life generally. It is a matter of chemistry. There are some people you can relate to, and others of whom a little goes a *long* way.

Moving to St. Louis

At the end of the school year, we got ready to come back to Missouri. I say "back" because we had often come to St. Louis for vacations and visits. We had always known we were going to settle there eventually, and by 1948 the city was almost like home. Shelby and his parents had moved to St. Louis from Tupelo, Mississippi, when he was seven years old, and he had grown up on the north side of the city on Dayton Avenue.

I was blessed with my in-laws. Daddy Freeman—Shelby Freeman, Sr.—was a Pullman porter and very active in the Brotherhood of Sleeping Car Porters. Mama Jennie—Jennie Barnes Freeman—was not employed when I knew her, though she had worked in a laundry years before. She was a lovely, sociable woman and an active member of Jamison Memorial CME Church on North Leffingwell Avenue, but Daddy Freeman did not

Mr. and Mrs. Shelby Freeman, Sr. (Mama Jennie and Daddy Freeman), at their fiftieth wedding anniversary.

join her there, and finally she gave up asking. He was hardworking and very frugal; by carefully saving his money and investing when a good deal came up, he had acquired a lot of north St. Louis rental property. On Sundays, he and his crew would take care of repairs, and later Shelby also participated. I asked Shelby to go to church too, but he never came with me unless it was a special occasion.

Shelby had gone to Vashon High School and afterward to Lincoln University, where he worked part-time driving for President Charles Florence. I am not sure how Shelby got this job, but I do know that he must have looked the part; his college friends always remembered that he was "the one with the suits." He was shy but a very good student—if it had not been for segregation, he probably would have become an engineer. Even so, he had many talents: mathematics, photography, and, a little later, computer technology.

After we arrived in St. Louis, we lived for a while with Shelby's parents at 3712 Finney Avenue. When one of Daddy Freeman's rental properties—a single-family house at 3129 Cass Avenue, a very nice neighborhood then—became vacant, we moved in. We took some time to get settled and get schools arranged, registering Pat at Dunbar Elementary School and Butch at a good day-care center, the Nursery Foundation. Then in September 1948, I traveled to Jefferson City to take the Missouri Bar exam, and on December 11, I was sworn in as a member of the Missouri Bar. At that point, I began looking seriously at what I was going to do next.

A Woman in the Law

Even before leaving Washington, I had taken steps to find a job in St. Louis. Belford Lawson, one of the leading black lawyers there and also the president of Alpha Phi Alpha, the fraternity Shelby belonged to, gave me the names of some major St. Louis law firms, and I wrote to them. They *still* haven't answered me. Over time, I have worked with some of those lawyers on committees, tried cases with them, and opposed them in court. When I tell them this story, they say to me: "We would answer *now*."

I also went to see Belford Lawson's dear friend David Grant, a distinguished St. Louis lawyer and civil rights leader, who was very active in Democratic politics and eventually served as president of the St. Louis NAACP. In 1931, he had been involved in an important protest in St. Louis, held at a north-side Woolworth store, and later represented black women arrested during the lunch counter sit-ins at downtown department stores. In the late 1930s and early 1940s, he worked with Thurgood Marshall on the Legal Redress Committee of the NAACP.

Dave Grant was a tall, good-looking man, articulate and well respected. He was very helpful to me, suggesting black law firms that I should contact—but when I did, and told them that I wanted to try cases, they let me know that was something they would not consider. They said, "Well, perhaps you could do *research*." They were willing to use me in the office, but that was about all. It did not take me long to realize that I was not going anywhere if I worked for them.

In those days, the law was absolutely a male-dominated profession—and the fact that I wanted to try cases made it all the worse. Since I am female *and* black, people will sometimes ask: "Mrs. Freeman, have you been discriminated against more because of your race or your sex?" And I say, "I don't know, but I have scar tissue from both." When I came to St. Louis, I could not join the Bar Association of Metropolitan St. Louis because they were not admitting black lawyers; when I did join, the meetings were dominated by men. For the few women, it was sometimes a lonely world. I did join the Mound City Bar Association and the National Bar Association, organizations of black lawyers. Margaret Bush Wilson, whom I also met during this time, was another pioneer in this area; she was admitted to the Missouri Bar before I was and had even run for Congress in 1948. She was also very active in the NAACP, becoming a member, then chairman, of the national board.

Establishing a Practice

So at this early point in my career, I went to Shelby and said, "I want to practice law in my own office." That meant I would need office space and furniture; it also meant I would need a lot of support. I had a husband and children, and many people in the late 1940s and early 1950s thought that a married woman with children ought to be staying home. But I believed that women had the right to choose a career and also be a wife and mother. I was fortunate that my husband agreed and that we had the help of Shelby's parents, who were devoted grandparents.

I asked around and found out that a lawyer, Virgil Lucas, who had an office on the second floor of the Jefferson Bank Building at Jefferson and Franklin, was moving to California. For the rent he was paying, around $50 per month, I was able to take over his office. So Shelby and I went shopping at second-hand stores to find a desk and other furnishings at prices we could afford. I hired a secretary/receptionist and had some business cards printed, then Dave Grant took me downtown and introduced me to the judges in the civil and criminal courts. I told them I was willing to be appointed to pro bono cases that would give me important exposure.

Either that same day or the next, one of the judges gave me my first appointment in a criminal case, asking me to represent a defendant who was charged with burglary for an incident in downtown St. Louis. As part of an urban-renewal effort, they were tearing down old houses to make way for the Plaza Square Apartments. A police officer caught my client dragging a bathtub down the steps of one building and shot him in the leg; he was in the hospital, under arrest. As I look back on it, I believe the judge was testing my skills as an attorney, because the man couldn't very well plead "not guilty." But I was able to arrange a plea bargain—my first—in which he was sentenced to serve only the time he had spent in the hospital.

Admitted to practice in the U.S. District Court for the Eastern District of Missouri, I was appointed to other pro bono criminal cases and also represented criminal defendants through my private practice. After about two years, though, I began to realize that criminal defense law was not what I wanted to do. Because of my family, I always had to make choices, particularly about what inconveniences I was willing to endure, and I felt that in order to be a good criminal lawyer, you had to spend more time than I wanted to spend on the job. Sometimes I would get a call at three o'clock in the morning, which was difficult for me personally.

There was another reason too. A little later, when I was appointed to serve occasionally as a provisional judge in the City Courts, I noticed a double standard that bothered me with respect to arrests. Every so often, I would be asked to convict a woman who was charged with prostitution, and I would ask the police or the prosecutor where the *man* was—but they had not arrested him! I told the police: "Don't bring me any prostitution cases in which you arrest the woman and don't arrest the man too."

So I decided to focus on the civil side of the law, as private clients began coming to my office. I remember the first man who walked in, probably on the second day I was open. He said he wanted a lawyer, and I said, "I am a lawyer." He looked at me, replied, "I don't want a woman," and walked out. Some people—even some *black* people—were also not interested in having a black lawyer; they felt that it would help to have a white lawyer. I was aware of that attitude, and every other black lawyer knew about it too. Today some black lawyers are getting the million-dollar lawsuits, but things were different then.

A few years later, I was in the process of successfully handling a race-discrimination matter for a black client, who wanted me to help him fight discriminatory roadblocks he had encountered in building up his construction business. One morning I was leaving the Civil Courts building, when I saw him standing at the elevator. I said, "Hi, what are you doing here?" and he answered, "I am waiting for my lawyer." He had a personal-injury case and had hired a white lawyer to handle it because he thought he would do better in damages! The fact that I could handle a civil rights matter did not translate as far as he was concerned.

Politics and Jordan Chambers

Now that I was getting established as a lawyer, I also wanted to become politically active. I was a Democrat through and through because I believed, as the party did, in certain basic rights: equal access for all, the need for social welfare programs, an end to segregation in education. Dave Grant knew how strongly I felt about taking part in politics, so he took me to see his friend, Jordan Chambers. Afterward, Dave always liked to say: "I told Frankie to do two things—get active with the Democratic Party and the NAACP—and she never looked back."

A group with prominent St. Louis political figure Jordan "Pops" Chambers (middle, smoking a cigar, with Frankie on his left) at the Club Riviera in St. Louis, ca. 1950.

Jordan Chambers, known to many of us as "Pops" Chambers, was a big part of the history of St. Louis. He smoked a cigar, wore big, broad-brimmed hats, and used colorful language. Along with owning the People's Funeral Home at Franklin and Cardinal, he also operated the Club Riviera on Delmar between Newstead and Taylor, a place where black jazz musicians came to perform. Politically, he had started out as a Republican, then switched to the Democratic Party in 1932 when Franklin Roosevelt was elected president. From 1938 until he died in 1962, he was committeeman of the Nineteenth Ward and very influential in Democratic politics. When black people wanted a job with the Democrats, the city, or the police department, they came to him.

After my meeting with him, I became active in the Nineteenth Ward Democratic Party. Within that small world of Democratic politics, I guess you could say that I was not in the innermost circle, but perhaps in the second circle of involvement. After a while, I was allowed into the "back bar" of the Riviera, the place where the insiders met to have strategy meetings—for example, if we were trying to get a public-accommodations bill passed by the board of aldermen and needed to tally up the votes we had. Outsiders couldn't get in; they had to stay in the "front bar" area, which was open to the public.

I also met some people who became dear friends for life: Howard Woods, the editor of the *St. Louis Argus*; Joseph Clark, president of the local NAACP and later Fourth Ward alderman, and his wife, Shirley; Leroy Tyus, who was an elected member of the Missouri General Assembly; and, of course, Dave Grant, who had been assistant circuit attorney but was then in private practice. Howard Woods and Joe Clark are dead now, and I miss them. We used to talk two or three times a week; we would call one another whenever something was in the news that we wanted to talk over. Now there is nobody for me to call and say, "This is crazy!"

One thing Pops Chambers was not sure about was having a woman run for elective office. While he had respect for what women could do, he was traditional in that way. At one point, I was interested in becoming a candidate for the Missouri House, and he was simply not ready. Later on, he changed his mind—and at that point *I* was not interested. But his view of women was very typical for that time, and as time went on, he did give me a lot of support in my career; I also learned a lot from him that has helped me throughout my life.

When it came to elections, for example, we all knew that Pops Chambers believed in accountability. First and foremost, his precinct captains had to carry their own precincts. Though I was not a precinct captain myself, that was still one of the lessons he taught me: Wherever you are in life, you must use your influence at *home* first, in the area where you live and work. In other words, I tell people that if you have something to do, you should "begin where you are *at*." Jordan Chambers also liked to say that once you decide to support someone, your word should be your bond.

Another thing he said was that sometimes you give people a job or do a favor for them—and that's the last you hear from them. In other words, they owe you something and maybe you ask them for support in some way, such as coming to a board meeting, and they never come. If you brought that kind of thing to the attention of Pops Chambers, he would say: "I'm going to take that tit out of his mouth." Now that's a colorful, slightly crude remark, but it gets the point across.

Finally, he used to say—and I still think about it—"Don't send a hungry dog to market." When you are selecting the person who will handle the funds for an organization, for example, don't choose someone who hasn't got any money. Or in the civil rights movement—and this has actually happened—make sure that the person negotiating the settlement doesn't end up with a job while the underlying policy remains the same. Don't choose somebody to work on an issue who can be easily shut up in that way. Whenever I am asked to recommend someone for a position, I think about this and consider what I know about them.

Participating in the NAACP

At the same time, I joined and became active in the NAACP. There I met three influential lawyers—Sidney Redmond, Robert Witherspoon, and Henry Espy—all Republicans, though that didn't matter. Whether you were a Democrat or a Republican made no difference when it came to civil rights cases because we all recognized that the issues transcended politics. These men were handling cases on behalf of the NAACP in support of plaintiffs who were challenging segregation and discrimination.

I was very impressed by all of them, and told them I wanted to volunteer to get involved in any way I could.

All three were very cordial and welcomed my help. Sidney Redmond, who had come from Mississippi originally, was the very picture of a Harvard man—scholarly, distinguished, articulate, a thorough gentleman; he lived on a private place, and you always had the feeling that he was quite well-to-do. He and Henry Espy, a Howard graduate, were law partners. As time went on, Henry consulted me, as he did many others, on a matter that was close to his heart. In the South, some blacks had managed to accumulate property, which was taken from them by whites in various ways, and Henry wanted to get back some of his own family's land in Florida through legal action. Unfortunately, I don't believe he was ever successful.

The third in this group was Bob Witherspoon, another Howard alumnus, who had his own practice, just as I did. As a Howard graduate, I came with good credentials, so even though they had all been practicing for some time, we could work together as peers. They didn't have time for spoon-feeding, so I had to get up to speed quickly. At that time, the Legal Defense Fund—known as the "Inc. Fund"—was part of the NAACP, though for the past twenty years it has been a separate organization. The four of us made up the St. Louis team, and there were teams like ours in many communities. Whenever we went to an NAACP convention, we met lawyers from around the country. In San Francisco, for example, there was a large NAACP organization that had a local team of Inc. Fund lawyers who were also involved in legal defense.

In those days, the NAACP was viewed as the salvation for black people in terms of legislative activities and litigation. In fact, every single major civil rights victory during that time was handled by the NAACP. One was the Lloyd Gaines case, in which the U.S. Supreme Court ruled that the University of Missouri School of Law, then a segregated school, would have to admit Gaines unless the state could offer him equivalent training elsewhere. There had been others, such as *Shelley v. Kraemer* in 1948, which effectively ended racially restrictive covenants in housing; and in 1954 there would be *Brown v. Board of Education*, which outlawed segregation in public schools. Whether you won or lost, the NAACP was there to challenge discriminatory treatment and discriminatory legislation.

Nationally, the NAACP had great leaders such as Walter White and Roy Wilkins, and the NAACP lawyers were civil rights giants. Charles Houston was the NAACP's chief counsel until he retired in 1938 and Thurgood Marshall took his place. The two of them had developed a campaign to attack segregation, starting with graduate schools, and to build up a history of anti-segregation decisions in the lower courts. By doing so, they could undermine the "separate but equal" decision—*Plessy v. Ferguson* of 1896—and lay the groundwork for the *Brown* decision. I worked with Thurgood Marshall and also with Robert Carter, an NAACP lawyer who later became a federal judge in Ohio. In all local NAACP cases, we always coordinated with Thurgood and the New York offices of the Legal Defense Fund, which he had established in 1946.

Locally, a number of us served on the NAACP Executive Committee. One was Henry Winfield Wheeler, a postal worker, member of the Missouri state legislature, and civil rights activist; a downtown branch of the post office is now named for him. He organized the picketing of the American Theatre, which ended its segregation in 1955. Beginning in 1956, Ernest "Cab" Calloway, who was a union official with the

Frankie hosts a dinner for NAACP friends and family, ca. 1977.

Teamsters, was also president of the local NAACP. His wife, DeVerne, was elected to the Missouri House of Representatives and became a very effective leader.

In those years, the Calloways became two of our closest friends, along with a group with whom we socialized regularly: Joe and Shirley Clark; Howard Woods; Irving Williamson, photographer for the *St. Louis Argus*, and his wife, Elizabeth; Jim Hurt, president of the Employee Savings and Loan Association; Reverend John Doggett; George and Bessie Draper; and Morris Hatchett, a lawyer and a Republican, but a good friend even so. We would get together—Shelby and I had the New Year's Eve party for the group at our home on Cass Avenue—and what fun we had.

Two other friends in this group were Marian and Charles Oldham, an interracial couple: Marian was African American, and Charles was white. Late on the evening of December 31, 1952, they were leaving our New Year's Eve party before the rest of the guests when Charlie was stopped by a policeman who asked what he was doing there. Here he was, a white man in a black neighborhood—and Charlie, who can laugh at the whole episode now, likes to joke that we even had red draperies on our front window, with the lights from our living room shining brightly behind them. I can only imagine what Charlie must have said then, but he was taken off to the police station. Marian came in and told us all, and Shelby, George Draper, and some of the other men went off to find Charlie. We knew that he had been questioned because he was part of an interracial couple; he and Marian had endured this kind of thing many times before. But we were angry, and we had some clout: George, for example, was then assistant circuit attorney. So they got Charlie out quickly, and I feel quite sure that that was one arrest the police officer was sorry he had made.

A Personal Blow

I had opened my practice in June 1949, and all this time our son Butch was up and about. Although he had worn a brace on his leg for a while after his illness, we thought he was doing well. That November, he was at the Nursery Foundation one day when they called to say he was falling down a lot. I went to pick him up and phoned Dr. Helen Nash, his pediatrician. I don't recall whether he began having convulsions then or a little while later, but either way he ended up at St. Louis Children's Hospital in critical condition. He survived, but he had to spend weeks in the hospital under Dr. Nash's care.

That was not only a personal crisis for us but also a financial one, because we did not have insurance to cover all these expenses. My father-in-law had to help us take care of our bills. As time went on, Butch's condition became less critical, but he did not get well. The doctors here told us that his original illness had been viral encephalitis and the doctors in Virginia had not recognized it. Now he had post-viral encephalitis syndrome. In counseling us, they said, "Why don't you have another child?"—this was the doctors' way of telling us that Butch would not survive.

He was blind and he was not able to walk; his communication skills were also limited because of severe brain damage, though he did recognize us. I think we all knew he would never become a "normal" little boy, but we did not admit it at first. Since he required custodial care, I got someone—Mrs. Irene Anthony—to help; my mother-in-law also provided some of his care. He was on constant medication to control the seizures. Dr. Nash was close to us; she made house calls at a time when doctors did not make house calls, and she was really our mainstay through all those difficult years.

Butch was a very lovable little boy, and I think we all grew in taking care of him during the nine years that he lived from that point on. We had to be careful that we didn't spend too much time with Butch and neglect our daughter, Pat, who also loved her little brother dearly. After Butch's condition had stabilized, I decided to continue with the practice of law, with my family's help and support. If this was the way things had to be, I could take care of Butch, Pat, my husband—do whatever I needed to do—and still be a lawyer. It was hard, and I had to pray continuously, "Lord, help me." And I would sometimes smile and laugh when I was not really laughing at all.

Professionally, I turned inward. In my law office, my clients did not know anything about my family life. I was very private about it. At times a client would tell me something that they thought was the "worst thing" that could be happening, and I would be thinking to myself, "You don't know, honey, you just don't know." For a long time, I also had to wrestle with guilt.

Frankie's two children, Pat and Butch Freeman, 1948.

I wondered, "Did I do something to cause this? What if I had been home all the time, the way mothers should be?"

My mother, who was very religious, wrote me a letter at that time in which she said, "The Lord brings us, in His own time, to the realization that He is always right and just in His dealings." I have come to this belief, too, but it is not easy. When I teach Sunday school once a month and the lesson is the book of Job, that is always a difficult thing to understand and communicate. My faith has been the basis of my survival in the midst of all this. It is not easy, but you can survive; you can get through it. God gave us Butch, and that is the way it was.

For Shelby it was different. He had never joined a church, but I really believe that some of his later reluctance had to do with Butch's illness. He did not see any reason for it. This was his *son*, whom he loved very much and wanted to get well. I was aware that he was handling it differently, but there was nothing I could do except try to understand.

Frankie at Washington Tabernacle Missionary Baptist Church on the occasion of her eightieth birthday.

Butch is one of the reasons I have always done whatever I can for children. For thirty years, I have been a board member of the Herbert Hoover Boys' and Girls' Club; I was a charter member when it was still only for boys. I am also on the steering committee of the Urban League Youth Development Fund. At my church, Washington Tabernacle Missionary Baptist, I was chair of the scholarship fund, which is named the Nance Scholarship Fund in memory of our former pastor, John E. Nance. I established the fund, and the first gift I made to it was a tribute in memory of my son.

The *Brewton* Case

Sidney Redmond had told me there was a case that he, Henry Espy, and Bob Witherspoon were just beginning to work on. When I read the details, I was very excited because it had substance and it related directly to my interest in civil rights. In my private cases then, I was getting mostly divorces—but this was different. It was a great opportunity, and they wanted me to be part of the team.

In 1949, Missouri law provided for racial segregation in public schools under the so-called separate but equal doctrine. The St. Louis public schools were also segregated, including the technical high schools: Washington Technical High School, which was for black students, and Hadley Technical High School, which was for white students. Under the law—the "separate but equal" doctrine—the curricula of the schools were supposed to be equal, so they each had a course in automobile mechanics. Then Hadley Tech instituted a course in airplane mechanics, to train white students in the basics of maintaining airplanes, but Washington Tech did not institute such a course.

Alton, Jr., Wesley, and Wilbert Brewton—three African American brothers who were close in age—were excited that a course existed in airplane mechanics. Their father, Alton Brewton, Sr., went to the principal of Hadley Tech to see if he could enroll them; he was refused, but he did not stop there. He went on to the school board, though I think he knew pretty well that they would refuse him too, and they did. He was told that his sons could take automobile mechanics. Sometime during this process, the NAACP began to assist him and advise him as to his possible remedies.

In those days, that was the way the local NAACP legal team often worked. Over the years, I have chaired many NAACP committees, and when people came to us we would advise them as to the steps they needed to follow before it came to a legal question, then we would expect them to follow the process we outlined. The NAACP would step in at what we considered to be the right moment.

This time, Mr. Brewton took the appropriate steps, then our legal team became involved. We filed suit in St. Louis Circuit Court in 1949, and there was a hearing, with Judge Aronson presiding, in which the board of education tried to justify their refusal to admit the Brewton brothers into the course. Their argument was based on the state constitution, but we argued that their refusal constituted a denial of the Equal Protection Clause of the Fourteenth Amendment of the U.S. Constitution and a violation of basic constitutional rights. Judge Aronson accepted that argument and agreed with it. He held that the board of education could not offer a course in airplane mechanics to white students without providing the same course to black students.

The board of education appealed that decision to the Supreme Court of Missouri, and over a period of weeks we had to file briefs and travel to Jefferson City to argue the case. Sidney Redmond presented the argument very eloquently for the NAACP; while my role was to simply act as co-counsel, I was certainly proud to be there. On the brief that we filed with the Missouri Supreme Court, my name appeared first because we were listed alphabetically—and from that time on, I always thought the alphabet was in my favor. But the lead attorney was Sidney Redmond, of course; all three of my colleagues had much more seniority in the practice of law than I did.

In a unanimous decision, the Supreme Court upheld the ruling of the lower court. They issued an order to the board of education saying that if they were going to provide a course in airplane mechanics for white students, they also had to do so for black students. However, the school board refused to do that. Instead, they simply removed the airplane mechanics program from the Hadley Tech curriculum.

Public opinion on this case was divided. Black opinion was on the side of the NAACP, as it always was when we were seeking to end racial discrimination, but some of the white public called us troublemakers. Keep in mind how pervasive segregation was at that time. Not only was it in the public schools but it was also in stores and restaurants, on the streetcars, in the movie theaters. I just did not go to the movies then.

As for the Brewton boys, they moved ahead with their career plans despite this outcome, and all of them received training in airplane mechanics during their military service. Alton, Jr., became a pilot and was killed in the Korean War. Wesley became an airplane mechanic in California. Wilbert also received his training in the Korean War as a radar technician and served for six years as manager for the Federal Aviation Administration at Spirit of St. Louis Airport. One time he was talking to his supervisor about the case and discovered that this man, who was white, had been a senior at Hadley Tech being trained in airplane mechanics at the time of the Brewton suit.

This case was especially significant for me because it was my first civil rights case, and it represented the beginning of my involvement with pursuing such cases in the courts. It was also a learning experience to see how far people would go to maintain racial segregation, and how short-sighted they were in undervaluing people on the basis of race. It didn't then—and it doesn't now—make any sense at all. Some of it was so ridiculous that you could almost laugh at it, except that it was not a laughing matter.

This case was also an illustration of how necessary it is for people like Mr. Brewton to stand up and not to acquiesce. People can be brainwashed into believing that they are inferior, that they can't do something—and that is a tragedy. Every time I speak I tell people what is expected of them: You do not acquiesce. When we pledge allegiance to the flag, we say "One nation, under God, indivisible, with liberty and justice for all." If that includes you, it means that you have a duty, a *responsibility*, to do all you can to make sure that everyone complies with those basic principles. So you don't sit down—you have to stand up.

Chapter Four

Fighting for Fair Housing in St. Louis

1952–63

URING THE EARLY 1950s, I was actively involved in my own practice, and with my three NAACP legal colleagues in St. Louis—Sidney Redmond, Henry Espy, and Robert Witherspoon—I went to the regional and national NAACP conferences. They kept us up-to-date on the NAACP's national effort to support litigation that would eliminate segregation in education and public housing. From time to time, we would also attend seminars to receive training in the constitutional issues that had to be raised in the courts.

Through those conferences and seminars, all of us doing civil rights work got to know each other well—forming a network of like-minded colleagues and friends that stretched across the country. And if you went somewhere, especially down South, to try a case, where would you stay? You would stay in the home of someone you knew through the NAACP.

In 1952, an important case related to racial discrimination in public housing came up in connection with the St. Louis Housing Authority, an agency established during the late 1930s under the Housing Act of 1937. Its role was to use grants and loans from the federal government to clear away slums in blighted areas and build housing for veterans and low-income families. Once this housing was built, the authority would also operate and manage it. With federal assistance, the authority had already built, and was then operating, two St. Louis housing projects.

On the north side, there was Carr Square Village, which had 658 low-income units for black families; on the south side, near the old City Hospital, was Clinton Peabody, with 657 units for white families. While the law did not require racial segregation in housing, there was a *practice* of racial segregation, and it was, in effect, supported by the federal government through the financial help it gave to these programs.

During World War II, the construction of low-rent housing projects was put on hold, but after the war the government gave money to local housing authorities for the construction of new units. So the St. Louis Housing Authority planned two more developments: the John J. Cochran Garden Apartments on North Ninth Street for white families, and the Captain Wendell O. Pruitt Homes at Jefferson and Cass for black families. In 1953 the Cochran project opened for whites, and the Pruitt project would open in 1955. Meanwhile, at a time when there was a serious housing shortage, Cochran offered the only new housing available for St. Louis low-income families—and it was designated for whites only.

Whites applied for Cochran, and they were accepted, but when blacks applied, they were told to wait for Pruitt. At this point, a group of prospective tenants went to the NAACP's Housing Committee, chaired at that time by Valla Abbington, and the committee tried to negotiate on their behalf with the housing authority officials. But those negotiations broke down, and the committee encouraged these people to come to us for legal assistance. We told them what their rights and options were; we also told them that we would help them if they wanted us to, and they said they did.

Robert Witherspoon and I agreed to handle the case for the NAACP. We were co-counsels, but I became the lead attorney because he was also lead counsel in another major case in federal court—representing defendants accused under the Smith Act of being Communists—and his time was limited. So I would argue the case with occasional help from Constance Baker Motley, the NAACP associate general counsel who had first joined the Inc. Fund team in 1945. She and I were already friends; we had met through the NAACP seminars around 1950. We had a lot in common from the start, professionally as well as personally. Like me, she was married, her husband was not a lawyer, and she also had a child.

After the case got underway, we were in communication by phone and letter on everything that transpired; as lead counsel on a number of other cases, she did a lot of traveling and would always stop off in St. Louis when she could. This case was a very exciting one for me, because it was the first major civil rights case I had argued.

Originally there were fifteen plaintiffs, some honorably discharged World War II veterans and some non-veterans, but all of them St. Louisans in need of low-income housing. They had placed their names on a waiting list—and many had been waiting for a long time. The housing authority kept their names on a separate list from the one they kept for white applicants and refused to consider them eligible for any housing that had been designated for whites.

On June 20, 1952, we filed a class-action suit, *Davis et al. v. the St. Louis Housing Authority*, in the U.S. District Court for the Eastern District of Missouri. I remember going to court with one of the motions and Judge George H. Moore looking at me and saying, "What is this case all about?" That was a chilling moment because it reflected the indifference of most people in the community—including some of the judges—toward racial segregation in housing.

In our suit, we argued that the housing authority's policy of segregated housing was denying these applicants equality of opportunity under the U.S. Constitution. That meant the authority was in violation of the due-process clause of the Fifth Amendment as well as the due-process and equal-protection clauses of the Fourteenth Amendment. We petitioned the court to issue a permanent injunction requiring the authority to stop making any distinction in housing based on race. As part of the settlement, we asked for $10,000 for each of the plaintiffs.

The answer of the authority to our petition came back on January 23, 1953. They admitted that the housing was intended for whites only. Like Clinton Peabody, they said, Cochran "was constructed in the neighborhood in the City of St. Louis predominantly inhabited by persons of the Caucasian race. The development contracted for was planned, constructed, and designed, so as to conform with the community pattern...." But they justified providing separate housing by saying that this segregation was "not for the purpose of discriminating arbitrarily against the

Frankie on the steps of the St. Louis Federal Courthouse with NAACP attorney Constance Baker Motley, October 1954. Frankie was arguing Davis et al. v. the St. Louis Housing Authority, *which ended segregation in public housing in St. Louis.*

Plaintiffs on account of their race and color"—rather, they had "a duty and responsibility under the law to preserve peace and order in the community for the protection and welfare of both races and, in the interest of public safety, to prevent racial conflicts and violence."

Next came the statement that was the most outrageous of all. They said: "The policy of operating separate housing projects for the two races is reinforced by recognized natural aversion to the physical closeness inherent in integrated housing from members of races that do not mingle socially." A *recognized natural aversion* between the races! Finally, they added that they didn't believe this lawsuit was instituted by "local Negroes" at all, but by outsiders who wanted to "stir up strife and racial conflict in a period of economic emergency and housing shortage." Well, talk about giving us motivation to continue! All I could think was, "Later for *you*." We knew it was going to be a hard road ahead, but we also knew the St. Louis Housing Authority had no real justification for its policies. In the school cases that were before the courts nationally, people could argue that there were state laws governing the policy of segregation, but in St. Louis there was no such law—just deep-rooted bias.

So we planned to hang in there, and we had the support of the NAACP and Thurgood Marshall in doing so. Other housing authority cases were proceeding elsewhere—in San Francisco, for example. But our case was unusual because the language of the pleading was so inflammatory. Since we knew the case would continue for a while and might well go on to a higher court, I decided to get the appropriate credentials in case it did. As a member in good standing of both the Missouri and Federal Bars, all I had to do was file this documentation and go to Washington, D.C., in 1952, where I was admitted to practice before the Supreme Court of the United States.

As the litigation proceeded, and motions were filed and argued, we lost a number of plaintiffs. Two were notified that there was suddenly a unit available for them in Carr Square, though they had been told at first that there was nothing—so those two dropped out, and others left for various reasons. By the end we were down to just one plaintiff—Sedell Calvin Small—and an NAACP award was eventually established in his name. Such tactics were all new to me then, but I know now that none of them were unusual in civil rights cases during that period. The opposing attorney would often say, "These are Communists. These are people who are trying to stir up trouble."

In the end, the defendants dropped the "natural aversion" argument and focused instead on the claim that the project should reflect the racial makeup of the surrounding community. To support their stance, they cited various community organizations that were also segregated, such as the hospitals, schools, churches, YMCA, and YWCA, and said that their policies of segregation showed there is "a custom long established in the local community of separate institutions." But they were making this argument at a time when these organizations were denying they were responsible for the system. The YMCA, for example, did maintain separate units, but it did not want to be cited as a basis here. The community was trying to move ahead, beyond this system, so this argument was not acceptable, and it was also not grounded in the law.

In October 1954, after two years of legal battles and delays, we finally presented oral arguments before Judge Moore. Connie had come to town the week before to prepare with me. The responsibility for reviewing the file, writing, and pulling my argument together was a major one. At the same time, of course, my family also required my attention. It was a big case, I was under stress, and I probably was not getting the rest I should have. But I did my homework, and I was ready.

In court, we argued that the housing authority had violated the equal-protection clause of the Fourteenth Amendment, citing the Supreme Court decision in *Brown v. Board of Education* and other federal decisions that declared segregation in housing illegal. Altogether, we were very pleased with the arguments and the presentation. In terms of the issues, in terms of the *law*, we felt that we had made our case.

Afterward, Connie and I had lunch, and she got on a plane to go home. I went back to my home too—and that evening I collapsed. All that had happened, all that stress, had finally caught up with me and knocked me out, but I didn't know then what was wrong. I was taken by ambulance to the hospital, where I spent five days. Some of the doctors said I was dehydrated, and I was certainly sick. From that time on, I have known that I need to watch myself whenever I am getting over-tired.

Finally, Judge Moore handed down a decision on December 27, 1955. The defendants were "forever enjoined" from "refusing to lease or rent to qualified Negro Applicants any units of public-housing projects...because of [their] race or color" and also from "maintaining a policy or practice of segregating tenants into such housing projects on the basis of the race or color of the tenants." All the costs in the case were charged to the defendants. The result was that we had effectively ended racial segregation in low-income public housing.

We were expecting the decision—I did not believe that Judge Moore could decide the case in any other way. The *Brown v. Board of Education* decision had eliminated any possible justification for deciding our case differently, but I was very pleased by the outcome. Connie was pleased, too; from that time, she sometimes called me, jokingly, "Frankie Freedom."

A New Front Line in the Battle for Fair Housing

After this decision, the housing authority's board of commissioners had to consider whether they were going to appeal. By then they had a new executive director, Charles L. Farris, who had come to St. Louis several months earlier and inherited this case. As he came on board, they were just combining the Land Clearance Authority and the St. Louis Housing Authority into one agency, now called the St. Louis Redevelopment Authority. They were also bringing on a friend of mine, Irvin Dagen, to serve as general counsel. His wife, Maggie, had been deeply involved in the struggle for equal opportunity.

On January 4, 1956, the authority's board of commissioners met in special session to decide whether they would appeal. In a unanimous vote, they chose not to go further; they also instructed their executive officers to move forward as quickly as possible to comply with the court's ruling. In an eloquent memo written on February 6, Charlie Farris told his employees that, although this change of policy came about as a result of court action, they were not to think that the housing authority was reluctant to comply with the decision. If the commissioners had been interested in delaying tactics, he said, they could have voted to appeal the decision and thus put off the policy change for another two years. The memo further stated:

> I want to state my own personal position…. Do the words of the
> Declaration of Independence and Constitution of the United States
> mean what they say, or are they empty and hypocritical pretense? Do
> the clearly stated principles of our various religions as to the equality
> of all men in the eyes of God have any application to our daily lives,
> or are they merely the stuff of which beautiful, but unreal, sermons
> are made?"

In late spring of that year, I got a call from Charlie Farris, who said,
"OK, Frankie, you beat us. You won the case. Now I want you to come
here and help make all these changes work." He offered me a job as first
associate general counsel of the combined agencies.

I was surprised by his offer but also very pleased because I had
received very little in legal fees for pursuing the *Davis* case. Over the
entire three-year period, I had been paid only around $1,000 for my
work, and because the case took a great deal of time, I did not have
much total income. In May 1955, on the recommendation of Jordan
Chambers, I had gotten a part-time job as assistant attorney general for
Missouri under Attorney General John M. Dalton. While it gave me a
small monthly salary for cases involving the collection of delinquent
state taxes, I was ready for a decent salary.

So I told Charlie, "I'll get back to you." First I talked to Irv
Dagen and then sat down with Charlie to discuss what I would be
doing. I knew I would have to give up my private practice, which I
had been involved in for seven years. By that time, I had moved my
office to my own home at 1209 North Grand, at the corner of Cook
Avenue. We had bought the house in 1953 because it was a large,
two-story, single-family house—big enough that I could have my
office and conference room on the first floor and living quarters on
the second. At that point, Pat went to Dunbar Elementary School,
but Butch still needed nursing care. So I decided to close down my
law practice and commit myself to working for the housing
authority.

Shelby made use of this larger place, too. For years, he had done photography, and now he decided to open his own studio in our home and work at it full-time; his darkroom was in the basement. His business, called Shelby Studios, grew quickly as he photographed weddings, celebrity appearances in town, and events such as the Y Circus, a big fund-raising event in St. Louis that showcased amateur and professional talent. He was also a local stringer for *Jet* and *Ebony* magazines. But, unfortunately, some people did not pay, so his income was erratic, and after three years he had to close the business.

Our move to Grand also meant that we were now living in the Eighteenth Ward, where Fred Weathers was the longtime Democratic committeeman. He was the counterpart of Jordan Chambers in that part of town, and the two men were very close allies, though they came from different backgrounds. Fred Weathers was a scholar, a Wharton School of Finance graduate, and a successful businessman who owned Marcella Cab Company. He was also active in the community, especially the YMCA; he belonged to the NAACP and the Urban League and contributed to many civil rights causes. I talked to Fred almost daily during those early years, but once I made the mistake of calling him around 9 A.M., and he told me, in no uncertain terms, that he did not want me to do that again. I am an early riser and, though I still call many of my friends at 7 A.M., I learned not to do that to Fred, no matter *what* happened.

Just as I was accepting the position with the housing authority, Fred came to see me and asked whether I wanted to be a candidate for Democratic Party committeewoman in the Eighteenth Ward. Earlier, when I had told Jordan Chambers that I might like to run for the Missouri House, he'd said, "Oh, no, no, no," and they picked a man as their candidate. So by the time they were ready for me, I had decided to do it another way. I still wanted to be involved in public-policy issues, but not as an elected official.

So I went to work for the housing authority under Charlie Farris. One newspaper article mentioned the irony of the situation, saying something like, "She beat them so they hired her." Other people only said, "Well, Frankie, you are smart and so are they." Though I was associate general counsel for the entire combined agency, Irv Dagen and I actually split the work: he did the legal work for the land clearance authority, while I did the legal work for the housing authority.

By then, the housing authority owned and operated not only Carr Square, Clinton Peabody, and Cochran but also the Pruitt and Igoe projects—all of which had been desegregated and were now serving the needs of an increasingly minority population. Day to day, I represented the authority in all its projects, which meant that I handled litigation, prepared contract resolutions, gave legal advice, and wrote legal opinions. We also had contracts with developers to build housing, and it was my job to review these contracts to make sure they were complying with the non-discrimination provisions. As a member of the National Association of Housing and Redevelopment Officials, I also represented the authority at these conferences.

It was challenging work. I learned about the role of government in operating national housing-policy programs and practice; I also learned a lot about monitoring contracts and development, construction and the legal requirements for it. But I had a lot of flexibility in my schedule. If necessary, I could work in the evening or start work early, so I could still go home and deal with things there when necessary.

My Delta Experience Begins

In 1950, I had taken the significant step of joining a sorority, Delta Sigma Theta. I had known about Delta while I was at Hampton, but we did not have sororities on campus then; I had also known about it when I was at Howard, but I had no time to join anything while I was there. My interest in Delta did not come from my mother, because she was a patron mother of another sorority, Alpha Kappa Alpha, which had a chapter in Danville that was active in the community. When I graduated from high school, I received a scholarship from Alpha Kappa Alpha.

But when I came to St. Louis, Inez Richardson—the wife of Scovel Richardson, a 1937 Howard law graduate who was then the dean of the law school at Lincoln University—invited me to become a member of Delta Sigma Theta. Delta was very well known as a national public-service sorority, founded in 1913 and composed of college-trained African American women. Today, we have grown to more than 200,000 members across the United States and abroad, and all of us "sorors" are still dedicated to social-action programs that will make communities more responsive to people's needs, make our country more accountable to its promise of freedom and opportunity, and help the deprived and oppressed achieve their full potential. Delta women have always supported campaigns and marches aimed at achieving justice and dignity for all people.

When I joined, I was probably the first lawyer to become a member of Delta's Lambda Sigma chapter. At that time, I still had my solo law practice, and this was an opportunity for me to meet other professionals, socialize, and enjoy my peers; it was also a chance to focus even more energy on civil rights and social action. When I went to national conventions, I found that I already knew women who were Deltas, and I also liked very much the new acquaintances that I made—Sadie Alexander, for example, the first black woman to receive a Ph.D. from the University of Pennsylvania. I ran into many of them again and again in my work on Democratic Party campaigns, since so many of them were politically active too.

One of the Deltas I most admired then and have ever since is Dorothy Height, who was national president when I joined the group; I had first met her when I was living in New York City, where she was an executive with the YWCA. Whether she is working on behalf of Delta or the National Council of Negro Women (NCNW), which she has served so well as national president, she has always been a persuasive, effective person, in a quiet way. She likes to knit, and I have seen her knitting quietly at a Delta convention—you would almost swear that she was asleep. But she was really listening intently; in fact, at that very convention, she heard a speaker mention something that gave her an idea—and she took that idea back to NCNW and implemented it.

She is also dedicated and persistent when it comes to things she believes in. Even now, when I stop by NCNW headquarters in Washington, I know that I had better have time to spend. Dorothy will say: "Oh Frankie, while you are here, would you look over this?"—and I find myself reading a contract or other legal document. But Dorothy has many friends who are glad to do such things for her, because she is so compassionate and has always given so much of herself to so many good causes.

Joining the Missouri Civil Rights Advisory Committee

The Civil Rights Act of 1957—the first federal civil rights act since 1875—had established a much-needed new agency, the U.S. Commission on Civil Rights. All of us in the civil rights movement were very pleased that it had been created. The commission was carefully constructed to be a truly bipartisan body; no more than half of its six members could come from each of the major parties. Its mandate covered several key points: investigating formal allegations that citizens were being deprived of their right to vote and have that vote counted, because of their color, race, religion, or national origin; collecting information about legal developments that constituted a denial of equal protection of the law under the Constitution; appraising the laws and policies of the federal government with respect to equal protection; and submitting interim reports to the president and Congress on its activities, findings, and recommendations.

I can best explain the functions and limitations of the commission by quoting from a decision of the U.S. Supreme Court early in the commission's history. "This Commission does not adjudicate; it does not hold trials or determine anyone's civil or criminal liability. It does not issue orders. Nor does it indict, punish, or impose legal sanctions. It does not make determinations depriving anyone of life, liberty, or property. In short, the Commission does not and cannot take any affirmative action which will affect an individual's legal rights. The only purpose of its existence is to find facts which may be subsequently used as the basis for legal or executive action."

The same act that created the commission authorized the formation of advisory committees to the commission in each state. So, in 1958, the Missouri State Advisory Committee of the U.S. Commission on Civil Rights was formed, and I was honored to be appointed as one of its charter members. My fellow committee members and I came from around the state and from diverse walks of life: educators, clergy, human-rights activists, attorneys, concerned citizens. Among the black leaders who served were Lorenzo Greene, a professor at Lincoln University, and my old friend Dave Grant, the St. Louis civil rights leader. But we were all citizen volunteers with a commitment to equal opportunity and the elimination of racial discrimination. With the help of a regional staff director, our role was to investigate and report on Missouri issues to the commission itself.

All the state advisory committees served as the "eyes and ears" of the U.S. Commission, holding meetings throughout the state and gathering information about issues. Over the years, the scope of the commission's inquiry broadened—from racial discrimination in voting rights and administration of justice, to gender discrimination, age discrimination, and denial of access to the handicapped—so ours did too. For example, in April 1961, while I was chairing the advisory committee's subcommittee on housing, we completed a report on housing problems of minorities in Missouri. Our findings showed, as we said in our summary, "that racial and religious discrimination and segregation in housing exist in varying degrees in all sections of the State; restrictions are practiced both in the sale and rental of housing." We had found many reports of discrimination among blacks, who were often excluded from suburban neighborhoods and forced to live in the older, blighted, urban areas. But we also had reports of discrimination against Jews in private housing sales and rentals. Of course, we passed these findings on to the commission office in Washington, D.C.

Without realizing I was doing anything wrong, I also released the report to the press and to Rep. Leonor Sullivan, who immediately put it in the May 9 *Congressional Record*. Then I got a call from the commission staff: "Mrs. Freeman, you are not supposed to release your report until we approve it," they told me. We had already held public meetings, and everybody knew what our findings were. But that experience taught me a lesson: protocol is protocol. And I never made that kind of mistake again.

The Little Rock Nine

The year 1958 was eventful for another reason as well. Not only was I appointed to the Missouri Advisory Committee, but I also became involved in the aftermath of the desegregation of Central High School in Little Rock, Arkansas. In 1954, the U.S. Supreme Court had handed down the *Brown v. Board of Education* decision, and I remember that when I heard the news I thought, "Hallelujah!" A few months earlier, I

Three of the "Little Rock Nine" meet in St. Louis, 1958. In 1954, the U.S. Supreme Court had ruled that segregation, or the legal separation of blacks and whites in public facilities, was illegal. Nine students, known as the "Little Rock Nine," became the first African Americans to attend Little Rock's Central High. Left to right: Jefferson Thomas, Thelma Mothershed, and Elizabeth Eckford.

had predicted that this would happen during a speech I gave to the League of Women Voters. I had told them, "The Court has got to declare that the 'separate but equal' doctrine is a fiction." I knew that the existing state of affairs could not continue.

The school board in Little Rock had been the first in the South to announce its intention to comply with this ruling, and in 1955 it adopted a phased-in plan that would begin with the integration of Central High in September 1957. But local opposition started to grow, and the NAACP filed suit, hoping to force immediate action. However, the courts endorsed the school board's plan, as segregationist sentiment increased. Of the seventy-five black students who applied to enroll at Central that fall, the board first selected twenty-five, then trimmed down the list to nine, who became known as the "Little Rock Nine."

While all this was going on, racial incidents were also taking place. A rock was thrown through a window at the home of Daisy Bates, president of the Arkansas NAACP; her husband was L. C. Bates, publisher of the *Arkansas State Press*, a black newspaper. On September 4, Daisy—who was a mentor to these nine students—called eight of them to say that a police car would drive them to school; but she did not reach Elizabeth Eckford, fifteen years old, who rode a city bus to school and tried to go in alone. Outside the school, Elizabeth came face to face with a hostile mob and National Guard troops who would not stand aside so that she could enter. When the other eight students arrived, they were not admitted either. On September 23, they finally managed to get into the school and continued to attend under protection of federal troops that President Dwight Eisenhower had sent in to enforce the desegregation. However, these students were subjected to harassment throughout the school year.

Of course, I was constantly aware of what was going on in Little Rock—as an active NAACP attorney, I was kept in the loop with respect to anything that happened nationally. All of us within the NAACP circle knew each other, and Daisy and I had become friends. In the spring of 1958, the NAACP determined that the Little Rock Nine students should go to school during the summer to catch up on their education, and, because of the climate in Little Rock, they wanted to get them out of the city. They decided to place them in a "safe house"— somewhere, within the NAACP family, where they would be in school and not subjected to any violence.

Daisy asked if I would take responsibility for three of these students, including Elizabeth. She was the one who had been most victimized, the one who had confronted the mob and had had things thrown at her. I would be a kind of surrogate mother to her—and I agreed to do it because I wanted to give these students a secure place to stay. We agreed that we would keep this whole matter within the NAACP circle; the public, and particularly reporters, were not to know what we were planning. So two girls arrived, Elizabeth Eckford and Thelma Mothershed, and one boy, Jefferson Thomas. The girls would stay with Shelby and me, giving Pat two "sisters" to enjoy; I arranged for Jefferson to stay with Mrs. O'Fallon, the mother of our friend and civil rights activist Marian Oldham. All three students were going to attend Hadley Technical High School during its summer session. Whenever they did anything socially, they all did it together—but only in the homes of NAACP friends. Wherever the students went, we knew exactly where they were.

They had only been in town for two or three days when I had to go to New York City for an NAACP committee meeting, and that is where I saw Daisy Bates, who first told me that Thelma had a heart condition. Daisy said, "Now, Frankie, if you see this happen or that happen…." So the day after I got back to St. Louis I took Thelma to my doctor and asked him to explain what had to be done. I also went to Hadley and arranged for her to use the school elevator, which was not ordinarily for students. At home we were always checking on Thelma to make sure she was all right, and she did fine. She became a schoolteacher in East St. Louis, and when she has been interviewed about this period, she has talked about the summer she spent with us.

Elizabeth came back the next summer, and this time Carlotta Walls came with her. All the while, Pat took her role as big sister seriously and spent a lot of time with the girls. Later, Elizabeth completed college at Central State University, coming back and forth to stay with us, and afterward she lived with us for several months before entering the military. She moved to Little Rock; Carlotta settled in Denver and went into real estate. But everyone involved was permanently affected by all that had happened, including Daisy's husband, who suffered serious economic consequences—and eventually lost his newspaper.

Deaths in the Family

The year 1958 was difficult personally as well as politically. In May, after his long illness, my son Butch died of pneumonia at eleven years old. He had been gradually weakening, but even so I don't think we believed his life was ending. Years before, doctors had tried to tell us that this would happen, yet we did not really accept it. The sense of loss we experienced is difficult to describe: we had to deal with all the pain of his death, and we also had to finally face up to the fact that we did not have a son. Pat, who was so devoted to her brother, took his death especially hard. At Butch's funeral, we asked the minister to keep the eulogy brief and have the service focus on music, which we all loved and found very comforting.

In October, we got word that my uncle Cecelius—for whom my brother Andrew Cecelius Muse is named—had also died. The next blow came soon afterward. After my mother's death in 1954, my father had told me, "Go home now, Frankie. I'm OK. I'm fine"—then, almost immediately, he had a stroke. He was ambulatory for a while, but over the next four years he gradually began to fail. When he finally passed away in December 1958, it was still a surprise but not the shock that my mother's sudden death had been. Since none of us were living in Danville then, we all went home for the funeral, and we felt the impact of his death as soon as we arrived—we were at home, but there was nobody there.

For a while, we kept the house on Ross Street as rental property, but afterward my brother Andy wrote to us outlining the things that it needed to maintain it. We decided to sell it rather than put a lot of money into it, and the buyers demolished it and built a new brick house on the site. So 215 Ross is still there, but it is not the house in which we grew up.

Muthoni

By 1960, I was still associate legal counsel for the housing authority, and in my private life, I was an active member of Delta. At that time, we had a large national program in the area of educational development, as well as an international program focused on Africa. In Kenya, for example, we had supported the establishment of a maternity clinic, so we invited Dr. Mungai Njoroge, the minister of health, to our national convention in Chicago to report on its progress. In his speech, he also touched on the need to educate young people and asked if any of us would open our homes to Kenyan students. I gave him my card and wrote on it, "I will," but I didn't think I would hear from him. When I told Shelby I had done that, he just gave me a *look*. "Why not take *two* or *three*," he said.

Next we received some forms on which we agreed to provide room and board. Then suddenly we got word that three young people would be coming—two boys and a girl—so I hurried over to the board of education to make arrangements for placing them in the public schools. Since I knew we could not take all three in our home, I contacted Virgil McKnight, head of Homer G. Phillips Hospital, and he offered to take in

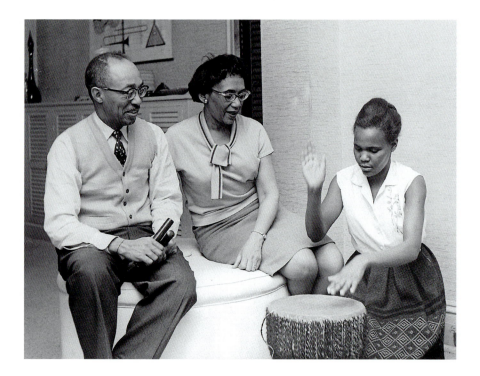

Shelby and Frankie with Muthoni Wainaina, the African student they sponsored, 1962.

one boy, Sebastien Wahome. A teacher in the public schools said she would take the second boy, James Muneo. But I did not hear anything about the girl who was supposed to stay with us until one day in September 1961, when I got a call from the airlines. They asked whether I was expecting a young lady from Kenya. I said, "Yes, but I haven't heard from her. I don't know when she is coming." They said, "She is here." Muthoni Wainaina, who was then fifteen years old, had arrived and was already in New York City, waiting to board her flight to St. Louis.

At least they *did* tell us when she was arriving in St. Louis, so Shelby and I were at the airport to meet her. I'm sure Muthoni was scared to death. I will never forget the things she brought with her: a little basket from her mother and a very nice letter from her father, Philip Wainaina, which had been written in English for him by someone else. In it he told us he was giving us his daughter to care for and protect, but I did not realize exactly what that meant until I had lunch one day with someone from Nigeria who told me, "Oh yes, he is really *giving* her to you." I had thought we were just providing room and board; I did not know that we were getting a foster child. It was a learning experience, but it was great.

That first year we had to work through the language and cultural barriers. At Thanksgiving time, for example, the teacher told all the students to draw a turkey. Well, everybody in America knows what a turkey looks like, but this was an African student who had absolutely no idea. So there were small problems along the way—some ups and downs—but Muthoni was a good student and finished Vashon High School in three years. Then I went to work and helped her get a scholarship from the Seven-Up Company so she could attend Central State University in Wilberforce, Ohio. Whenever she was at home, all the African students from the university would stop by our house and visit; they called me the "African Den Mother."

At Muthoni's graduation in 1968, I was the commencement speaker. That was the time when students were staging disruptions at graduation ceremonies. Although they did not riot at Central State, I do remember sitting on the stage and watching one of the graduates bring out a big trash can, start a fire, and urge his fellow students to come up and burn their gowns. However, I also noticed that was something he didn't do himself, because he had a rented gown and would have had to pay for it. Instead, he removed his gown, folded it, and placed it under the podium.

While Muthoni was at Central State, she met a young civil-engineering student, Peter Kiburi Karimi, who was studying at Purdue University. He was from Kenya too; in fact, the two families lived within miles of each other but had never met. On August 31, 1968, Muthoni and Peter were married at Berea Presbyterian Church in St. Louis, and the reception was at our home. Afterward, they moved to Madison, Wisconsin, where Peter finished a master's degree in water-resources management and Muthoni completed a medical-technology course before they returned to Kenya. Recently, Peter retired after serving as that country's chief water-resources engineer, and Muthoni still works as a biochemist at Kenyatta Hospital. They have four children, all of whom are in the United States. Their oldest son, Karanja, also lived with us while he attended college.

Shelby and Frankie host their annual Christmas Eve open house for colleagues, friends, and international students, ca. 1980.

In 1957, Shelby and I had started having an annual Christmas Eve open house for our colleagues and friends. Once Muthoni came to live with us, our traditional welcome to international visitors at our annual Christmas Eve party always included students.

A Trip to Hayti, Missouri

Meanwhile, the civil rights struggle was continuing. A month before the 1960 presidential election, sit-ins were taking place in more than one hundred southern cities. Martin Luther King, Jr., had moved to Atlanta to head the Southern Christian Leadership Conference, and in May 1961 two groups of Freedom Riders embarked on a bus trip through the South; both trips ended in Alabama, where the buses were attacked by mobs of angry whites.

Just weeks after the presidential inauguration, I was taking my own bus ride to southeastern Missouri. At that time, I was vice chairperson of the state advisory committee, vice president of the National Council of Negro Women, and an active member of Delta Sigma Theta. The Hayti Alumnae Chapter of Delta had invited me to be its keynote speaker for a Founders' Day program on Saturday, February 4. The only other way to get there was by car, and I decided it was too far for me to drive alone. So I boarded a Greyhound bus that morning; it was a beautiful day, and I remember repeating the slogan, "Ride the bus and leave the driving to us." The seat was comfortable, and I relaxed, using the time to look over notes I had prepared for my speech. When we arrived at our first rest stop, in Flat River, I got off with other passengers, went into the restaurant, and on to the ladies' room.

As soon as I got there, I could sense a chill around me. A female employee, who later identified herself as Gloria, called out rudely, "The colored use another entrance." I proceeded to the door marked Ladies, where a white female customer stood blocking my passage. She repeated what Gloria had just told me: "Colored can't come in here. You have to go to the one on the other side." I stood and looked at her.

Then the bus driver came over, and I told him I wanted to lodge a complaint. I checked for his badge and asked for his name, which he did not give me. I then looked at the woman who was still blocking the door and thought to myself, "If I push my way in here past her, I will be arrested, and my sorors in Hayti will not have a speaker for their Founders' Day celebration." So I turned around and went back to the bus. That is, I know that I *walked* back to the bus, that I *walked* back up the steps and over to my seat. But emotionally, I *crawled* back to the bus and up the steps. While most of the passengers were still in the restaurant, I went to the restroom on the bus, and when I sat down again, I began rewriting my speech for that day to reflect what had just happened.

The next stop was in Sikeston. I got off the bus and found a public telephone so I could call Shelby back in St. Louis. I asked him to contact our friend, attorney Charles Oldham, who was also a member of the Congress of Racial Equality (CORE), and tell him that I wanted to file a complaint against Greyhound and the restaurant in Flat River as soon as I returned to St. Louis.

When I arrived in Hayti, my sorors were there at the bus stop to meet me, and I told them about the incident. I knew, of course, that denial of access to places of public accommodation had been pervasive in earlier years; I had even experienced such things myself—but I was not prepared for such a confrontation in Flat River, Missouri, in February 1961. As a member of the state advisory committee, I had already participated in meetings held in southeast Missouri. However, I had always traveled by car and had never before encountered any problems.

When I returned home on Monday, I contacted Charlie Oldham, who did file a complaint with Greyhound. Articles appeared in the *St. Louis Argus*, the city's leading black newspaper, about the incident. Soon Greyhound issued an apology and said that the restaurant had agreed to change its policy. Two weeks later, a group from CORE checked out the restaurant and found that the separate facility for "colored" had been eliminated.

1963: A Pivotal Year

Beginning in August 1963, the St. Louis chapter of CORE organized an important demonstration, lasting seven months, to force the Jefferson Bank and Trust Company on Washington Avenue to hire black clerical employees. Although I had closed my account at Jefferson and supported the CORE members I knew best, such as Charlie and Marian Oldham, I had only a very minor role in the protest. I was not on the picket line and was never arrested, but I did read and prepare some legal documents related to the protest. I have always felt that whatever role people played in the civil rights movement—whether on the front lines or in the background; in CORE, NAACP, or any other group—it took all of us to make a difference.

Certainly, we all shared the aspirations expressed so beautifully by Dr. Martin Luther King, Jr., in his speech on the steps of the Lincoln Memorial on August 28, 1963. Although I knew the march on Washington was going to take place, I had just come back from an NAACP convention in Chicago and felt I could not take time off work to go. However, when I got home that evening and heard the speech on television, I remember that I was lifted up, as was everyone else who heard it, by the eloquence of Dr. King's language. It was one of the masterpieces of all time, and it had an impact. But there was also so much more work to be done.

Chapter Five

Joining the U.S. Commission on Civil Rights

1964-65

IN 1960, I WAS A SUPPORTER OF THE DEMOCRATIC PARTY, but I was not involved in partisan political campaigns because, as a housing authority employee, I was restricted by the Hatch Act from engaging in such activities. However, I was still active in efforts to enact state and federal civil rights laws, and I had some national visibility because of my work in civil rights. So the St. Louis City Democratic Committee included my name on the list to be invited to President John F. Kennedy's inauguration in January 1961.

Several national officers of Delta Sigma Theta were also invited, and we all stayed in a block of rooms at the Gramercy Inn, including President Jeanne Noble, Geraldine Woods and her husband, and Lena Horne, an honorary Delta member, who was there with her husband, Lennie Hayden. We attended the inauguration, and I was among the crowd when President Kennedy gave his famous address, "Ask not what your country can do for you...." He was articulate, handsome—there was an aura about the Kennedys. I remember that, to celebrate this happy occasion, I had bought an evening gown—in red, the Delta color—for the inaugural ball that evening.

Since the day was quite snowy, we decided to watch the other events from our hotel room. My friends say that my hair "always needs some attention," and I recall Lena Horne rolling up my hair as we sat in front of the television, doing our make-up and getting ready for the ball. Lena Horne is a lovely, down-to-earth person; it is easy to forget that she is so famous. As an entertainer, she had to endure much discrimination, and she would talk about those things with us sorors privately. But when we went to the receptions, people would flock to her, and she was as gracious as could be with them. I always enjoyed watching her perform and would be sure to do that whenever I could, then go backstage afterward and visit.

Two longtime friends of mine were staff members of the Democratic National Committee: Ethel Payne, a well-known journalist for the *Chicago Defender* newspaper; and Louis Martin, deputy chairman of the Democratic National Committee and a columnist for the newspaper, as well as its former editor-in-chief. Occasionally, they would write to me

A reception following Howard University's conferring of an honorary degree upon Lena Horne, May 1979. Left to right: Dr. Geraldine Woods, Frankie, Lena Horne, and Jewel LaFontant.

Frankie (second woman from right), President John F. Kennedy (back turned), and Jacqueline Kennedy (first woman from right).

and ask for an analysis of some position or situation related to blacks in St. Louis and Missouri.

Meanwhile, I was pleased to see President Kennedy become the first president to state in unequivocal terms the morality of the cause for which black leaders and their supporters had fought, with little success, since Reconstruction. In his civil rights message to Congress in February 1963, President Kennedy said, "Therefore, let it be clear, in our own hearts and minds, that it is not merely because of the Cold War, not merely because of the economic waste of discrimination, that we are committed to achieving true equality of opportunity. The basic reason is because it is right."

On November 17, 1963, I was asked to go to the White House to meet with Lee White, associate counsel to President Kennedy. He told me that I had been recommended for nomination to the U.S. Commission on Civil Rights. At that point, there were two vacancies, created by the resignations of Spottswood Robinson, who had recently been named a

U.S. District Court judge in Washington, D.C., and Robert Storey of Dallas, president of the Southwestern Legal Foundation, who had resigned because of illness in his family. Traditionally, one slot on the commission had been occupied by an African American, and the departure of Spottswood had left that position vacant. It would be a special honor to take his place. Not only had he been a member of the Howard law school faculty when I was a student there, but he was also a member of the national NAACP legal team and one of my role models.

We talked about my work, my interest in civil rights. Although we did not discuss it, I knew that President Kennedy had said he was going to appoint more women to executive positions, so the fact that his administration was considering me was probably part of this program. I also knew that the commission had never yet had a woman member; to this point, it had been made up of five white men and one black man.

I returned to St. Louis knowing that I was under consideration—and I was excited about it. As a member of the Missouri Advisory Committee, I was very familiar with the commission, the issues they were dealing with, and the challenges of their work. It was an honor just to be considered for such a high-level position, but I also was aware that there was a lengthy, difficult route to such an appointment.

Just a few days later, on November 22, I was at the hairdresser's when the news broke about President Kennedy's assassination. It was devastating, just devastating. I came home and made dinner—went through the ordinary routine of living—while listening to the radio and watching television. We *all* went through the routine, but we were grieving, we were mourning. As far as the nomination to the commission went, I thought that whole possibility was at an end.

New Presidency, New Possibilities

Then Lyndon Johnson became president. Until then, I had known of him only as a powerful senator from Texas and then the vice president. But apparently, Margaret Price, vice chairperson and director of women's activities for the Democratic National Committee, first submitted my name to President Johnson very soon after he took office, and he began to consider me for the Civil Rights Commission.

In a 1997 biography of Louis Martin, *Walking with Presidents*, author Alex Poinsett said that President Johnson had called Martin to ask about me only two weeks after becoming president. According to Poinsett, Martin gave me a strong recommendation, then suggested that the president check my credentials further by talking to Robert Weaver, NAACP official and head of the Housing and Home Finance Agency; he knew me because NAACP lawyers and professionals working to end discrimination met together regularly throughout the year.

On February 14, 1964, our local newspapers announced that President Johnson was coming to St. Louis as part of the city's two hundredth anniversary celebration. He was to give an address at a gala

Frankie looks on as Lyndon Johnson delivers a speech in downtown St. Louis while campaigning for the U.S. presidency, 1964.

Bicentennial Birthday Party, sponsored by the Chamber of Commerce, at the Chase-Park Plaza Hotel. Shelby and I bought our tickets to attend.

The morning of the celebration, I was at my desk at the St. Louis Housing and Land Clearance Authority, where I was still associate general counsel, when the phone rang. It was Jack Valenti of the White House staff. He said, "The President is going to be in St. Louis and would like to meet with you this afternoon." I quickly grabbed a yellow pad and began writing down the instructions that he gave me. The dinner was at 6:30, and President Johnson wanted to see me at 5:00 in his suite at the Park Plaza. I said, "Yes, I will do that." It was all a shock, but I had no doubt that I would be there.

As soon as we hung up, I called Shelby, who was then a digital computer programmer for the Department of Defense in St. Louis. I told him I was going home to get myself together and asked whether he would try to leave work early so we could dress and still be there on time. I am not sure to this day whether he believed the phone call was for real, but he did all that. We left in plenty of time to drive from our home on North Grand to the Chase, which is at the corner of Lindell and Kingshighway—ordinarily a fifteen-minute drive.

President Johnson had arrived in town earlier that day and made other stops before proceeding to the Chase, so his motorcade was en route at the same time we were—and that meant something we had not anticipated: heavy traffic. It was just horrendous. Shelby tried everything imaginable to get there, but when we reached the corner of Maryland and Kingshighway—about a half block away from the hotel—he had to let me out so I could walk the rest of the way. There I was, on the north side of the intersection, with crowds of people between me and the entrance. When I tried to cross over, a policeman stopped me and said: "You cannot cross." I said, "But the president wants to see me. I have an appointment with the *president*." He looked at me—here I was, an African American woman, saying I had an appointment with the president! I showed him the instructions I had written down, he went to talk with his supervisor, then he came back and said: "Follow me."

We made our way through the Chase Hotel to the Park Plaza lobby, then, in front of the elevator, the policeman said, "Have a seat there."

While I was waiting, the publisher of the *Globe-Democrat* newspaper, Richard Amberg, walked by and smiled. Leonor K. Sullivan, congresswoman from the Third Congressional District whom I had known for fifteen years, came by and whispered, "Congratulations, Frankie," then got on the elevator and went up. I found out later that President Johnson had asked for her opinion of me as a prospective appointee, and she had given me a strong recommendation.

So I sat there waiting, getting more nervous and numb, until some time after 5:00 when they took me up to another floor where President Johnson had his suite. As I got off the elevator, I saw a line of Secret Service men, and one of them ushered me into a parlor. Then Jack Valenti came in, apologized for keeping me waiting, and said the president would be with me shortly. As I recall, I was wearing a gray satin, after-five coat.

After a while, they took me into the next room—and there was the president, big and tall, standing in the doorway. He smiled and invited me to sit down on the sofa. I was so overwhelmed that I clutched the lapels of my coat and did not let go! He could probably see that I was nervous, so he began talking, telling me that he had heard a lot about me: my work as a civil rights attorney, my efforts to eliminate discrimination in housing. He said he had checked me out with Roy Wilkins of the NAACP and Whitney Young of the Urban League, and they had said good things about me. "But I did not tell them which position you were being considered for," he said, "because I knew they had some *man* to recommend." He was nominating me, he said, to be a member of the U.S. Commission on Civil Rights. Needless to say, I was surprised and delighted. I replied, "Thank you, sir, it is an honor."

However, I also told him that I knew who the commissioners were—they were all academics—and didn't know whether I would fit in with that group. "Oh, Mrs. Freeman," he said, "I think you can handle all those *deans!*" The commission then included four men from leading universities: John A. Hannah, president of Michigan State University; Erwin N. Griswold, dean of the Harvard University School of Law; Robert S. Rankin, professor of political science at Duke University; and the Reverend Theodore M. Hesburgh, C.S.C., president of the University of Notre Dame. So President Johnson was just lumping them all together as deans!

As we continued to talk, he asked me a few questions, including this one: "Mrs. Freeman, you're going to have an FBI investigation, and I want to know whether you belong to any organizations that I need to know about." I thought frantically and said, "I'm a Baptist!" I knew he was talking about a communist group or something like that, but I couldn't think of anything along those lines. He just smiled at me and said, "I think that will be all right."

The more we talked, the more I relaxed, and we could discuss some of the things I had done as well as President Johnson's anti-poverty program. What a great society we would have, he said, if our nation undertook a war against poverty with the same commitment and resources that we would marshal if we were attacked by outside forces! He said he viewed poverty, too, as an enemy of our country. We were having a good conversation, when suddenly there was a knock on the door. Apparently, we had been talking too long because an aide was there saying, "Now, Mr. President...." So President Johnson said that I would hear from him, and I left the room, walking on air. I was impressed, overwhelmed, honored, proud.

I went down to dinner and sat at a table with some colleagues and friends, including Jim Hurt, president of the Employee Savings and Loan Association, and Evelyn Roberts, president of the St. Louis branch of the NAACP. Fred Weathers and other prominent Democrats were nearby. But nobody besides Shelby knew that I had come from a meeting with the president until the next morning, when there was a front-page story in the *Globe-Democrat*. Then they all called me with flippant remarks like, "My gosh, we had dinner with you and you didn't even mention this!" Fred Weathers said, "You never talk anyway." I didn't. I sometimes traveled to Washington and when I came back Fred would say, "What happened?" and I would answer, "Nothing." I always told him that if there were things he needed to know I *would* say something, but he must have thought I should have told him things at times when I did not.

The Nomination

The newspapers were speculating about what position I might be appointed to, and the Civil Rights Commission was one of the agencies they mentioned, though there were others as well. An article in *The*

Washington Post later said that the president had also considered the Department of Health, Education, and Welfare, the Federal Housing and Home Finance Agency; even a diplomatic mission for the Department of State.

Two weeks after my interview, I was watching a presidential press conference on television when I heard President Johnson announce that he was nominating two people for the U.S. Commission on Civil Rights: Frankie M. Freeman and Eugene C. Patterson, who was a Georgia native and editor of the *Atlanta Journal-Constitution* newspaper. That's how I found out—and it was absolutely wonderful.

Afterward I got official notification, along with many phone calls. A *Washington Post* reporter called and asked about my experiences at civil rights protests; I mentioned that I had been involved some years earlier in the picketing of the American Theatre in St. Louis. When the article came out, it was entitled "Lady Lawyer from St. Louis: She Fought in Court and Streets," and it implied very strongly that I would do that again, whenever the need arose. The commission staff called me and said: "Please, Mrs. Freeman, do not talk to any more reporters." They were concerned that I might not get through the Senate and wanted me to be quiet until I was confirmed.

At this point, local and even national newspapers were commenting on my nomination. The Danville newspaper covered it, and I discovered later that several people from Danville had written to the president; these letters, coming from home as they did, still mean a lot to me. One was written by Ruth Harvey Wood, an attorney and president of the Southeastern Lawyers' Association; another was from the Danville chapter of the Hampton Alumni Association.

The *St. Louis Post-Dispatch* and the *St. Louis Argus* both endorsed my appointment, as did some St. Louis leaders: Fred Weathers; Nannie Mitchell-Turner, president of the *Argus*; and DeVerne Calloway, who knew what it was like to be a black woman in government. Margaret Bush Wilson was laudatory, but realistic. She said, "I think it's a fine recognition of Mrs. Freeman's ability and services—I just wish it paid a salary." Others also wrote letters or telegrams on my behalf, including my former boss, Missouri governor John M. Dalton; Dorothy Height, president of the National Council of Negro Women; and several NAACP officials, including Evelyn Roberts. Geraldine Woods, president of Delta Sigma Theta, wired on behalf of Delta's thirty-five thousand members, and she also must have asked the regional directors to get busy, because letters came in to the president from black women around the country.

I still had not spoken with Charlie Farris about my job—the one that *did* pay a salary—with the St. Louis Housing and Land Clearance Authority. To meet the requirements of this new position, I would need time off to attend commission hearings in different parts of the country, but fortunately I had accumulated some leave time. From 1964 to 1970, I would use all of that, plus my upcoming vacation and leave time, to go to Washington or do anything I needed to for the commission. Charlie Farris was nice about all of this, even though, as time went on, the commission was critical of some things that pertained to urban renewal.

Confirmation by the Senate

On July 28, 1964, Eugene Patterson and I appeared at a hearing, held by the U.S. Senate Judiciary Committee's subcommittee on constitutional rights, to consider our nominations. Since President Johnson had first announced our names, these hearings had repeatedly been delayed; the Judiciary Committee was headed by Senator James O. Eastland of Mississippi, who was known for dragging his feet on civil rights matters.

This subcommittee had nine members, and three southerners were among them, including the chairman, Senator Sam J. Ervin, Jr., of North Carolina. Fortunately, one of the other members was Senator Edward V. Long of Missouri, who made laudatory comments, but also—perhaps to make my appointment more palatable to the southerners on the committee—characterized me as a moderate, praising "my judicious temperament and objectivity" and my "skills in conciliation." Interestingly, the two southern committee members besides Senator Ervin did not attend this hearing.

The other Missouri senator, Stuart Symington, came to the hearing and filed a statement on my behalf. In his book about Louis Martin, author Poinsett mentions that both Missouri senators had been miffed that the White House had not followed the usual recruitment protocol and consulted them about my nomination. The "two slighted legislators" demanded to know, Poinsett said, "'Who told the president? Where did he get this name? Who's making these appointments anyhow?" When Representative Leonor K. Sullivan appeared next to speak in favor of my nomination, she made clear that the president *had* consulted her, questioning her at length about my appointment.

Then Senator Kenneth Keating, a Republican from New York State, said he hoped that my nomination would be quickly approved, and finally Senator Ervin turned to me for a comment. I said that I was "honored by the appointment of the president. It is my opinion that the work of the Civil Rights Commission is one of the most significant that this country faces today. I will bring to it my best."

No one had any questions or presented any opposition to my nomination. Senator Ervin concluded: "I take it, by the presence of a number of persons here today, that they are in favor of the confirmation of the nomination." Then he moved over to Eugene Patterson for a brief consideration of his credentials. The hearing had begun at 10:30 A.M. and ended by 11:55. After it was over, Senator Ervin came to me and said, "Mrs. Freeman, after this interview I am impressed with your credentials, but I cannot vote for you because I don't agree that there should be a U.S. Commission on Civil Rights." I only said, "I understand what you are saying, Senator. You do the best you can." What he said was not a surprise to me. Behind the scenes, other southern senators were angry that the composition of the commission, originally made up of both civil rights proponents and southern conservatives, was breaking down. They thought President Johnson was interested only in strengthening the commission's support for civil rights.

After further delays, our appointments were confirmed by acclamation: mine on September 15 and Eugene Patterson's, as the commission's new vice-chairman, on October 19. I'm not sure what Senator Ervin did, whether he stayed home or what; there was no roll-call vote. But anyway, I was officially a member of the U.S. Commission on Civil Rights—the first woman to have the job. At that time, there were few women in high-level federal positions, so I felt especially honored. But my appointment was more than an honor: It was a challenge and an opportunity for service. I also felt it was a great privilege to serve in such distinguished company.

While I was waiting for the Senate to consider my nomination, I was invited to attend all the commission meetings as a commissioner designate; of course I couldn't vote, but at least I was involved. I also attended the annual retreat—and one of the first things I found out was that the commissioners usually found a place where the men could enjoy fishing. I remember somebody saying to me, "Well, they won't be going fishing now," because, whatever people thought of me, they did not imagine that I went fishing. The first retreat I attended was at the Land o' Lakes in Minnesota, a retreat center owned by the University of Notre Dame.

Frankie and family after the U.S. Commission on Civil Rights swearing-in ceremony, 1964. Left to right: front row—Shelby, Frankie, and Pat; back row—Cassie ——, Brenda and Elaine Peebles (nieces), Eric Muse (nephew), and Maceo Snipes (cousin).

My swearing-in ceremony was held at the commission office at 1121 Vermont Avenue in Washington, D.C. In the front row were Nicholas Katzenbach, acting attorney general, and LeRoy Collins, director of the Community Relations Service, both of whom were charged with helping to enforce the Civil Rights Act of 1964. Members of the commission were there, my family all came, and a friend whom I had met through the National Council of Negro Women—Judge Marjorie Lawson of Washington, D.C.—swore me in. I am only sorry that I did not think to remove my hat.

The State of the Commission

When I joined the commission, it had just come through a difficult period in which important staff members had left and the general counsel had resigned. But President Kennedy had assured Chairman Hannah of his commitment, and soon positive things began to happen: William T. Taylor became general counsel and other key staff members were added. Of course, President Kennedy's assassination threw all these things into doubt, but President Johnson said he wanted the commissioners to stay in office and continue making progress. At the same time, he also promised that he would move ahead on the civil rights legislation envisioned by President Kennedy.

He was true to his word. In February, the U.S. House of Representatives passed the Civil Rights Act of 1964, and in June the Senate passed the bill by a narrow margin. Civil-rights organizations, including CORE and the NAACP, saw the Civil Rights Act as a major step forward, since it created an Equal Employment Opportunity Commission (EEOC), made employment discrimination illegal, and barred federal assistance to state or local programs that practiced discrimination. Through a provision in Title II, the public-accommodations section of the bill, the Civil Rights Act also made it illegal to deny access on the basis of race, color, or religion to such public places as restaurants, theaters, hotels, and lunch counters.

There were also things that it did not do or that created controversy. While the Civil Rights Commission had recommended appointing federal registrars wherever there was clear evidence of discrimination in voting, this act merely said that voters with a sixth-grade education should be allowed to vote and any registration tests should be administered in writing. The act also extended the life of the commission for four years—but this led to debates in Congress. Southern senators complained that the commission was stirring up trouble, while northern senators thought it was helping to secure equal rights for all Americans.

We *needed* constructive solutions during the summer of 1964. In Mississippi, an organization called the Council of Federated Organizations (COFO)—consisting of CORE, the NAACP, the Student Nonviolent Coordinating Committee (SNCC), and the Southern Christian Leadership Conference (SCLC), along with Mississippi civil rights groups—had launched a voting rights project called "Freedom Summer," which recruited college students to register black voters in Mississippi in time for the 1964 presidential elections. Three civil rights workers—Andrew Goodman, a New York City college student, Michael Schwerner, and James Chaney, both civil rights workers—were reported missing and later found dead.

In the midst of such incidents, the commission asked for an increase in funding to $1.76 million in order to undertake new workshops, reports, and inquiries. Chairman Hannah went before the House Appropriations Committee to defend the commission and its budget request, arguing that most of the provisions of the Civil Rights Act of 1964 had actually come from the commission and its work. In the end, we got $1.5 million, enough to fund our staff of 116 people. Then, in February 1965, President Johnson nominated Bill Taylor, formerly the general counsel, to become the commission's new staff director. His appointment came just in time, since we were investigating a matter that the commission had postponed looking into: a voting rights hearing in Mississippi.

The Mississippi Hearing Begins

Early in 1963, Attorney General Robert Kennedy had opposed the idea of holding a Mississippi hearing because he feared it might interfere with the legal case his department was bringing against the governor for resisting the admission of James Meredith to "Ole Miss." So the commission instead prepared a report that described the shocking conditions in the state and brutal acts of intimidation and violence that were preventing people from registering to vote. But the commission had never wanted to give up on holding a full-scale hearing, and now, early in 1965, we finally decided to go ahead. Our plan was to focus on five Mississippi counties and look at the problems there.

Throughout January, our staff—a wonderful group, made up of black and white members—worked hard to line up witnesses who could testify to such problems. Of course, they also made sure these witnesses would be protected in case of possible reprisals. In order to produce a constructive report, we also wanted to include any evidence of progress in promoting civil rights, so the staff also looked for balance in the testimony. As always, they did their work in cooperation with the state advisory committee, which in this case had already endured threats and harassment. A committee member from the Tougaloo College faculty told us that she drove out of her garage one morning and found tacks thrown all over her driveway.

The hearing schedule was a two-part process. First, we would hold an executive session at which we would hear privately from any witnesses who could be "defamed, degraded, or incriminated" by their testimony; that is, when an allegation was made against someone, they had a chance to appear during this session first to explain their action. After that, we would hold the public session, which had two parts as well: the first dealing with voting rights and the second with administration of justice. As usual, Bill Taylor would question the witnesses, and the commissioners would each have a turn after he finished. We set a date for beginning, February 10, 1965, and a place: Jackson, Mississippi.

Suddenly, Attorney General Nicholas Katzenbach asked for the hearing to be postponed. Echoing the argument that Attorney General Robert Kennedy had made two years earlier, he said that the Department of Justice was building a case against the Mississippi men accused of killing the three civil rights workers, and that if we held the hearing now it might interfere with that case. However, we did not want any delay. Some of us felt that the department's concerns were not justified; we also believed we had a public responsibility to do this kind of fact-finding, and we all knew this hearing was important because President Johnson was preparing his proposal for a new voting rights bill, which he would submit to Congress in March. With the agreement of Bill Taylor, who was still the general counsel until his appointment as staff director was confirmed by the Senate, we voted unanimously to hold the hearing over the attorney general's objection.

When I arrived in Mississippi that February, I got my first hint that the commissioners could face risks at these hearings. Some staff members picked me up from the airport to drive me to the hotel, and on the way there I saw a fruit stand and asked to stop off for a minute. They said, "Mrs. Freeman, are you crazy?"—they were afraid to stop because something might happen. For that reason, they always made sure that security was tight. We had federal marshals watching us, though we never really knew who they were. Only once did I know—at a hearing in Boston, where the situation was so tense that they assigned a marshal to accompany me wherever I went.

At this hearing in Mississippi, there was something I wanted to do even before the executive session began. Four black churches where people had tried to register to vote—Pleasant Green, Christian Union, St. John the Baptist, and Cedar Grove—had been burned in Canton, Mississippi, about twenty miles from Jackson, and I decided I wanted to go there. How could anybody burn a church, I wondered? I had to see it for myself. Before the hearing began, I asked the staff to find me a car so I could drive to Canton. They said, "Oh no, we don't think that would be safe." Then I said, "Well, look. You *get* me a car. I am *going* to Canton, Mississippi"—and they did.

The next morning, when I got ready to leave, I found that commissioner Griswold and his wife were coming along, and some staff members were joining us too. We saw those burnt-out churches, and I cannot describe how moving it was. More strongly than ever, I realized that we were in trouble as a nation and had to do something about it. The others were also affected—so much so that from then on, whenever the commission had a hearing, we always arranged for a site visit, if at all possible.

"I Do Intend to Vote"

So we opened our hearing with a two-day executive session, followed by a five-day public session starting February 16 in the Veterans Administration Center. During that public session, we heard thirty subpoenaed witnesses: they were black and white, people who had been denied the right to vote, as well as state officials. The whole hearing was televised nationally to a wide audience. That was a blessing, because not only did people across the country learn many lessons, but Mississippians also saw and heard things that they had never known about before. Some *did* know, of course; some were even the ones *doing* these things. But there were also many decent people who had not realized how bad it was.

Chairman Hannah began the hearing, as he always did, by introducing the commissioners and describing the duties of the commission. He said we were limiting our inquiry to two areas—voting and law enforcement—and to events that had happened since January 1, 1964. We were not calling

Frankie (left), with John Hannah (center) and Eugene Patterson (right), facing President Johnson during a White House meeting of the U.S. Commission on Civil Rights, 1965.

witnesses from counties involved in cases instituted by the Department of Justice, he said, but we were collecting information from other areas, and we would be reporting it to the president and Congress with recommendations for corrective action. Then he asked me to read the rules that would ensure the hearings were conducted in an impartial manner.

Our first visitors had not been subpoenaed. As a courtesy, we had sent letters to Mississippi governor Paul B. Johnson and Mayor Allen C. Thompson of Jackson, describing what we were doing, and both responded that they wished to come before us and make brief statements. Governor Johnson began by saying:

> The Civil Rights Act of 1964 is the law of the land, and Mississippi knows it. Most Mississippians do not like the new law. They are convinced that its passage was unwise and unnecessary. Some of them will challenge its constitutionality in the courts, as is their right. But resistance will be confined to such accepted legal processes.... I wish to assure all Americans that Mississippi will continue to be the most law-abiding state in the nation.

Mayor Thompson spoke next, extending to us "one of the most cordial welcomes you have ever had anywhere." He was anxious, he said, "to give you the facts as they really exist." These were powerful statements, and we were pleased with them. When the governor talked about Mississippi as "the most law-abiding state," we hoped that if there were allegations, if there were *victims*, the Mississippi political leadership would do something about it.

Other witnesses—black leaders such as Charles Evers (brother of Medgar Evers, who had been murdered)—were more pessimistic about change. They testified about the voting-registration campaign underway in Mississippi and the reprisals against prospective black voters: the burning of homes, the bombing of churches, etc. Governor Johnson, they argued, was only acting in a conciliatory manner because his state was on display nationally. Aaron Henry of the NAACP said that he was "not at all convinced that this great change of heart he is now expressing is a genuine change. You wait until the commission goes back to Washington."

Then we heard about actual incidents from witnesses such as Mrs. Unita Blackwell of Mayersville, in Issaquena County, Mississippi, a COFO worker who was trying to get people to go to the courthouse and register to vote. She said that, since their drive had begun, around 150 black people had tried to register, but only 9 or 10 had succeeded. She herself had tried three times, even though she had only an eighth-grade education. The first time, an election official gave her a dense, complex section of the state constitution, section 182, which began this way: "The power to tax corporations and their property shall never be surrendered or abridged by any contract or grant to which the State or any political sub-division thereof may be a party, except that the legislature may grant exemption from taxation in the encouragement of manufactures…."

The procedure for the board of elections in Mississippi was that if you were black you had to read and write, and interpret the Constitution to the satisfaction of the registrar. So after Mrs. Blackwell had tried her best to interpret this section, she asked how soon she could find out whether she had passed. The registrar said she could come back in thirty days. She did that and found that she had *not* passed; she was told she could try again in two weeks. At that point, she went back and was asked to interpret a different section, section 111—another difficult part, dealing with the judicial sale of land. On her third visit she got yet another section, and this time she passed. As she explained it, "This time she [the registrar] helped, because of all, you know, so much had been going on and everything, all the civil rights and Justice Department, everybody running in. And she was all upset."

In questioning Mrs. Blackwell, Bill Taylor asked whether she intended to vote now that she had been allowed to register. "I do intend to vote…. Because it is very important to have the people represented, and I wants somebody to represent me," she said. Were things changing in Issaquena County? he asked. "Well, I hope so," she replied. "But, you know—well, the people now are still afraid." She described an incident with a white man in a pickup truck who had threatened her. But "you just get to the place where you know it's going to happen but you've just got to stand up and got to do something," she said. I then asked her whether she had ever seen any white people trying to register during the various attempts she had made. "No. They was just in there drinking coffee, and…you know, just standing around," she said.

All this was not a surprise to me; I knew this kind of thing was going on—I was just hoping that we could put it on record, make it public. But the courage of people like Unita Blackwell was inspiring. She was a remarkable person who became deeply involved in the political process, and in 1977 she was elected the mayor of Mayersville—the first black mayor elected in Mississippi.

Another witness was Guthrie Hayes Hood, a white man who was the circuit clerk and registrar of Humphreys County, Mississippi. Bill Taylor questioned him first, asking him, "How many Negroes are registered to vote in your county?" He said he did not know. Bill then referred to some figures, given at an earlier session, which showed that 68.3 percent of the 3,344 voting-age whites in that county were registered to vote, and none—*not a single one*—of the 5,561 black people. Mr. Hood replied that he did not know whether those figures were correct or not, but he did say that, during the previous five years, sixteen blacks had tried to register— and none had passed the test.

When it was my turn to question him, I asked Mr. Hood what his level of education was; he said he had gone to high school through eleventh grade. I asked whether *he* had ever been tested on his ability to interpret the state constitution—and he admitted that he had not. So how did he select the sections to be used in testing applicants, I wondered? He said he had each section of the constitution typed on a 3"x5" file card, and applicants were assigned the sections in numerical order. If one got section 100, the next person would get section 101, and so on. He claimed this was a fair system, and that he had never chosen "hard" or "easy" sections to give to specific candidates.

Commissioner Griswold, dean of the Harvard University School of Law, also questioned Mr. Hood, asking him to interpret one of these sections himself: section 182, the same one that Mrs. Blackwell had first been given. Mr. Hood began to read it, but Dean Griswold stopped him and asked him to *interpret* it, not read it. On the advice of his attorney, he declined to answer on the grounds that his answer might incriminate him. Dean Griswold said—and I think he was voicing the feelings of us all—"I find it a little hard to see how citizens of Mississippi are expected to interpret the section if the registrar is unable to do so, and he is the person who grades the interpretation which is made." I don't think Mr. Hood felt very comfortable when he left that hearing.

Other witnesses at this hearing described the same kinds of voting abuses. Mrs. Mary Oliver Welsh of Humphreys County testified that, when she tried to register, Mr. Hood had "hollered at me and scared me" and "told me I was going to get in trouble and he wasn't going to give me no commodities [government food assistance]." She said she had lived in that county for thirty-one years but had never before tried to vote because "I was scared to go see." Bill Taylor asked why she wanted to vote, and she replied, "Well, I want to vote for freedom. That's all I know."

In the second part of the public hearing, we turned to the administration-of-justice side of things, where we would inquire into the burning of the four black churches and allegations that people were intimidated while trying to unionize black workers at Mississippi plants. We heard from witnesses such as Alfred Whitley of Adams County, a janitor at Armstrong Tire and Rubber Co., who had driven home one February evening and found two cars blocking the road to his house. When the drivers got out and came back to his car, they were wearing hoods and carrying guns, pointed at him. After tying his hands, they drove him to a swampy area, pulled his clothes off, and whipped him. They said they were doing it because Mr. Whitley, who was black, was a member of the NAACP; he denied that he belonged to any organization except his church, but they beat him anyway. Finally, they told him to run and then fired shots at him, but just out of flashlight range, he dropped on his stomach and avoided their fire. He said he had recognized one of their cars: it belonged to a white coworker, who had recently asked him about his views on education for black children. Mr. Whitley had told all this to the local sheriff, but no arrests were ever made.

Another black man from the same county, Leonard Russell, told the story of a fire-bombing at his home. Apparently, at his place of work—the International Paper Company in Natchez, Mississippi—he had filed a grievance on behalf of himself and some black fellow workers because all the facilities at his plant were segregated except the water fountains. Since he knew there might be trouble, he had asked for police protection and even moved away from his home. But this incident had happened anyway.

There was also testimony from people who were trying to keep these kinds of things from happening, so there was some progress. Still, this was my first hearing, and I was galvanized by it. I thought: "We've got to stop this kind of thing; we *have* to change this." I also knew that I had a special role to play on the commission as a "twofer." There was one *woman* and I was she; there was one *African American* and I was she. I felt that I had to speak out—I had to, and I did. Friends of mine and fellow members of the NAACP would remind me, from time to time, "Don't forget now who you are"—but they said it jokingly, because I was never in danger of forgetting.

I was very aware all the time, of course, that my fellow commissioners were people of stature, such as Erwin Griswold. But I also tried to remember what President Johnson had told me: "You can handle those deans!" And, though we were a bipartisan group, there was never any division along party lines during the entire sixteen years that I was on the commission. We had some differences, and some commissioners were more conservative than I was; in an oral history about these years, Eugene Patterson said:

> ...since I was, I suppose, the most conservative member of that commission—my tangles were with [Mrs. Freeman] but they were, again, pro forma. I was expected to be the nay-sayer, the man who questioned any radical move. And she was expected, being black, I think, by her people to fight me. So out of these frictions, we did have some good arguments, but we also wrote better reports than we would have if we'd just done unquestioned things that the staff handed to us.

But there was never any division among the commissioners on the basis of political interests. Erwin Griswold, Father Hesburgh, Robert Rankin—they were all very forthright in their questions. Everyone on the commission was committed to equal opportunity. Still, I like to think that the brothers and sisters whose stories we were hearing sometimes looked over and, seeing my black face, felt a little more confident about talking to us. However, I don't think that was a major factor; the commission itself was what they mostly thought about. When Chairman Hannah raised a question, they would feel the power of that as much as when I did.

At times we were all appalled by what we heard, but you could not get so caught up in despair that it would take over, because you couldn't be effective then. Sometimes I would put my hands together and just say, "Lord." Tears might come to my eyes, but then I would remember I was on camera and brush that aside. And you had to keep in mind that, even though we were hearing some horror stories, people were getting on top of this, and change was happening.

Frankie joins Lady Bird Johnson on the campaign trail in St. Louis, 1964.

Until much later, I did not realize the effect these hearings were having on my family, how worried they were about my safety. Even if I had known, it wouldn't have stopped me from doing what I did, but I might have called home more often to say, "I'm OK."

Reporting to Congress

In May, following this hearing, we released a report, "Voting in Mississippi," and sent it to the president, the president of the Senate, and the Speaker of the House. Our letter said that the commission "has found that Negro citizens of Mississippi have been and are being denied the right to vote in violation of our Constitution." We traced the history of voting rights abuses in the state, particularly the literacy tests and the poll taxes, and described the reprisals that black citizens faced when they tried to register. All together, we said, this systematic exclusion meant that Mississippi had the worst voting record among blacks of any southern state—only 7 percent of voting-age blacks were registered to vote. The Civil Rights Act of 1964, we said, had not really improved this situation; more would have to be done.

So we also presented recommendations for change. First, literacy tests and poll taxes should be abolished. Whenever there was a pattern of discrimination, voters should be allowed to register under federal registrars, and federal poll watchers should be appointed to supervise elections. Second, we recommended new training programs in adult education, literacy, and community action, administered by government departments.

Some of these findings became part of the Voting Rights Act of 1965, a strong piece of legislation that appointed federal examiners to fight discrimination in voter registration throughout the South. On August 6, 1965, in the rotunda of the Capitol where Abraham Lincoln had signed the Emancipation Proclamation, President Johnson signed into law this act, which someday may be looked on as the Magna Carta of southern blacks. As he said then, "So, let me now say to every Negro in this country: You must register. You must vote. You must learn, so your choice advances your interest and the interest of our beloved nation."

In 1969, I appeared before the Sub-Committee on Education of the U.S. House of Representatives to speak on behalf of the extension of the Voting Rights Act of 1965. What I said then is something that I believe in still. I said:

Mr. Chairman, at a time when one hears of so many demands from so many groups, I speak in support of what surely must be the most modest demand of all, the demand of American citizens to elect their representatives and officials in the greatest democracy in the world. At a time when there is so much talk of law and order, I speak to remind the Congress of its sworn duty to uphold the highest law of the land, the Constitution of the United States. That Constitution guarantees to all citizens the right to vote, regardless of race or color. Negroes in the south, under the protection of the

A retreat of the U.S. Commission on Civil Rights at Land o' Lakes, Wisconsin, June 1966.

Voting Rights Act, have at last begun to exercise the right to vote which for so long was illegally denied them. Next year will mark the one hundredth anniversary of the Fifteenth Amendment. In that centennial year, the promise so long broken and so recently redeemed must not again be denied. I urge you to extend the Voting Rights Act.

All this happened decades ago, but it is sad to realize that some of these issues are still current ones. During the 2000 presidential election, for example, we had problems with regard to votes being counted and people not knowing how to vote. So the problem of the participation of everybody—"the consent of the governed," as our Declaration of Independence says—is still with us.

The good news is that, in Mississippi, things have improved greatly with respect to African Americans voting. At one point in the recent past, Mississippi had more black elected officials than any other state. It has a way to go in terms of average income and the number of citizens below the poverty line, but at least those atrocities that we heard about in 1965 are no longer happening today.

The U.S. Commission on Civil Rights gives Clarence Mitchell a citation as "101st" senator. Left to right: Frankie, Arthur Flemming, Clarence Mitchell.

Chapter Six

An Era of Civil Rights Action

1966–71

THE MISSISSIPPI HEARINGS WERE MY INITIATION into the commission and its work. Over the coming years, I participated in many other hearings by the full commission, as well as hearings conducted by subcommittees, which I sometimes chaired.

Late in 1965, President Johnson asked the commission as a whole to do an in-depth study into the problem of race and education. Our goal, he said, was to lay "a firm foundation on which local and state governments can build a school system that is color blind." This assignment was different from others that the commission had undertaken; in the Mississippi hearings, for instance, we had limited our inquiry to a single state. This time, we would be doing a comprehensive study of racial isolation in public schools across the United States. Our chairman, John Hannah, said this was "perhaps the most important assignment this commission has ever undertaken."

The issue of racial segregation in public education is one that I have always felt strongly about. Some people believe that the races should be separated in schooling. Among whites, there are some who think they are superior; among blacks, there are those who talk about black power and are antiwhite. I reject all of that. I believe that the Constitution is for all of us, that we are *all* created equal. Because I am a Christian, I also think our survival requires that we get to know and respect one another—and that starts with our educational system.

Through 1966, the commission worked to fulfill its charge from the president, holding hearings on this subject around the country. In 1967, we issued our report, "Racial Isolation in the Public Schools," which outlined the problems caused by racial isolation and suggested specific remedies, such as substantial investment in new facilities. In conclusion, we said: "The central truth which emerges from this report...is simply this: Negro children suffer serious harm when their education takes place in public schools which are racially segregated.... When they become adults, they are less likely to participate in the mainstream of American society, and more likely to fear, dislike, and avoid white Americans."

I wholeheartedly agreed with all of that and with our further statement that the very existence of ghettos is a legacy of slavery and persistent discrimination, including the discriminatory practices of the housing industry over the years. Yet I wanted to go further. I felt that it was particularly important for me to express my views since, unlike any of the other commissioners, I could speak from personal experience. So I prepared a supplementary statement that said, in part:

> As the principal value-bearing institution which at one time or another touches everyone in our society, the school is crucial in determining what kind of country this is to be. If in the future the adults in our society who make decisions about who gets a job, who lives down the block, or the essential worth of another person are to be less likely to make these decisions on the basis of race or class, the present cycle must be broken in classrooms which provide better education than ever, and in which children of diverse backgrounds can come to know one another. None of the financial costs or the administrative adjustments necessary to bring about integrated quality education will be as costly to the quality of American life in the long run as the continuation of our present educational policies and practices. For we are now on a collision course which may produce within our borders two alienated and unequal nations confronting each other across a widening gulf created by a dual educational system based upon income and race. Our present school crisis is a human crisis, engendered and sustained in large part by the

actions, the apathy, or the shortsightedness of public officials and private individuals. It can be resolved only by the commitment, the creative energies, and the combined resources of concerned Americans at every level of public and private life.

After I wrote this, I showed it to Father Hesburgh, who concurred with my opinion. Commissioner Griswold did not see it at that time, but later he told me he would have concurred as well.

After our report came out, the public reaction ranged from shock to denial. I knew it was not going to be popular. Some people misunderstood, and there were also deliberate distortions. People claimed we were saying that a black child had to sit next to a white child to get an education. Within the black community, some said we were criticizing the all-black schools, while we were actually challenging the unequal and inadequate resources of the all-black schools.

We were anxious to see what the White House would do about these findings, but there was mostly silence from the administration. I don't know why—perhaps events in Southeast Asia were preoccupying President Johnson then. I made sure that key civil rights leaders received a copy of the report, with special attention to my supplementary statement. I traveled to New York and met with Roy Wilkins of the NAACP, Whitney Young of the Urban League, and Dorothy Height of the National Council of Negro Women. They received it well, and all three organizations endorsed our findings.

In March 1968, a year after our report came out, the National Advisory Commission on Civil Disorders, known as the Kerner Commission, issued its landmark report on race in America. Their findings echoed what I had said: As a society, we were moving toward two societies, one black and one white, separate and unequal. White racism was the factor they held as essentially responsible for the explosive mixture that had been building up in U.S. cities for the past twenty years. Overall, they stressed a message we had also tried to convey: "What white Americans have never fully understood—and what the Negro can never forget—is that white society is deeply implicated in the ghetto. White institutions created it, white institutions maintain it, and white society condones it."

U.S. Commission on Civil Rights, 1965–66.

So what happened to that warning? In March 1969, an assessment of the crisis we had all described was made by Urban America and the Urban Coalition and published in the report "One Year Later." It found that the cycle of poverty had been slowed by the counter force of a strong economy, but even so, the cycle of dependence, measured by the number of welfare recipients, had accelerated, and job discrimination was still pervasive. In summary, the report said, "The Nation has not reversed the movement apart—Blacks and Whites remain deeply divided in their perceptions and experiences of American society…. There has been some change, but not enough."

A year after that, I gave a speech in South Carolina at Delta's Founders' Day observance and shared some of my feelings about this bleak picture. I said then that we are all "diminished as long as there is hunger and discrimination in this land." To change things, I said, we need builders, dreamers, and doers among our people: "teachers who take the extra step to help students overcome the failures of other teachers; lawyers who plead for the poor and victims of injustice; government officials ever alert to see that laws against discrimination are enforced." We still need those kinds of people today.

Becoming Delta President

In 1967, Delta Sigma Theta was about to hold an election for a new national president to succeed Geraldine P. Woods. As usual, a national nominating committee brought in a slate—but for some reason they did not bring in my name, even though I was first national vice president. Instead, the nominee for president was Thelma Daley from Baltimore, who had been a national Delta officer. At first I was hurt, and the St. Louis chapter was upset, too. My friends here told me that I should run anyway at the biennial Delta convention, which would be held that year in Cincinnati, Ohio.

So the St. Louis chapter launched a campaign on my behalf—with leaflets and mailings to the membership, just like any political campaign—and Annie B. Brooks was my campaign manager. On the first day of the convention, I was nominated from the floor by the delegate from St. Louis. The balloting is on the morning of the third day, and the result is announced at the closing banquet, which ends the convention.

No one is supposed to know the results until the banquet, but word gets around, and I had already received several congratulatory phone calls before the banquet began. I was trying to get dressed; I had bought this special ensemble, off white, with a long coat and matching dress. By the time I got downstairs to join the procession into the banquet, I was late, honestly late; I am *never* late, but I truly was that time. However, some people thought I was coming in late on purpose—that I knew I was elected and was trying to make an appearance. Jeanne Noble teased me later that I had "flaunted in," but I replied that "I *don't* flaunt." The Deltas seated there who knew the outcome applauded me, but most people did not yet know.

Now Sadie Alexander was general counsel at that time, so she was on the program. Of course, she already knew the results, and when she got up to speak, she gave it all away without realizing it. As she began, she said, "Madam chair, madam this, madam that, and *madam president-elect, Frankie Freeman*." So by the time they called for the report of the election committee, everybody knew already, except the ones who hadn't been listening. I had won decisively. After the banquet, there was a lovely party to celebrate.

On the morning after the banquet, Jeanne approached me right away and said, "Frankie, I suggest that you name Thelma as chair of National Projects," which is one of the most important committees, since it oversees all the Delta programs. I said "I'll do it," not only because Thelma was a friend, but also because she was a brilliant person and a very good worker. So I went to her immediately and asked whether she would accept that position. She said she would, and we hugged and cried. A few years later, Thelma was elected the seventeenth national president herself.

That Cincinnati convention had a number of highlights for all of us, including a special commendation from Vice President Hubert H. Humphrey for Delta's "Teen-Lift" program, our annual career motivation project aimed at disadvantaged youth. Barbara Jordan, the only African American member of the Texas state senate, was the banquet speaker, and she called us to action: "We do not want racism and factionalism and fear and hatred to destroy our land…. Join in helping to bring about the full light of day."

Frankie with Barbara Jordan at the Delta Sigma Theta national convention, 1971.

So I had become fourteenth national president, and that meant I was wearing several hats, since I was also serving on the commission and working at my housing authority job. But I felt that I could intermesh these roles, bringing my other experiences to bear on my leadership of Delta and drawing upon my interest in individual responsibility to create productive change.

During my presidency, I continued the Five-Point Program that had been developed under Jeanne Noble's leadership. The original five points—Library Service, Job Opportunities, Delta Volunteers for Community Service, International Project, and Mental Health—evolved over the years, becoming Educational Development, Economic Development, Physical and Mental Health, Political Awareness and Involvement, and International Awareness and Involvement. Implementing this program requires legislative support, and I wanted every Delta to become more involved in her government at the local, state, and national level. Throughout my presidency, my emphasis was on public policy; with the riots, protests, and other civil rights issues so prominently in the news then, I wanted to respond to the needs of that time.

We started a program at our regional conferences in which every soror would write a letter to her congressman on some issue, often civil rights, then we would march together with the letters to the mailbox. Later presidents have continued that and developed it into Delta Days at the Capitol, in which we now write letters to members of the U.S. Congress and even visit their offices. I worked to broaden the scope and size of Teen-Lift, first established in 1962, by including both black and white teenagers from diverse backgrounds and, with the help of a grant from the Danforth Foundation, by adding a four-day sensitivity training workshop to the program.

As president, I tried to stress my belief that each individual is personally responsible for participating in social action. A lot of people don't even know who their state representative or congressman is. I believe that you should not only know who that person is but also be vocal enough that he or she knows who *you* are. Delta members still come up to me today and say I helped to get them involved, and I am proud of that.

I also hope that I served as a role model for the women of the organization who are all college educated and trying in many cases—as I had in my life—to juggle career and family.

In 1968, with the next convention due to take place the next year in Baltimore, the national board met in St. Louis. For one of our sessions, I scheduled a meeting of the board with some women of Pruitt-Igoe whom I had met through my position at the housing authority. I wanted the Deltas to see that these women had exactly the same desires that they had. At first, the session was a little awkward, but it didn't take long for barriers to disappear and the sisters to start talking. Whatever our background, it was clear that we all wanted the same thing: a better future for our families. Through the years, board members have come to me and talked about that meeting, saying, "I remember when you took us to Pruitt-Igoe."

The Baltimore convention was one of the largest to that date, with twelve hundred Deltas and their families attending—and my call to that convention was "One Nation or Two," based upon my supplemental statement in the "Racial Isolation" report. They engraved my phrase "two separate and unequal nations" on a medallion, and even now, whenever I go to a convention, somebody will still have it. That year, I was also reelected for another two-year term of office. During the previous year, the country had enacted fair-housing legislation; of course, the Voting Rights Act of 1965 had also been passed. So this time, my emphasis as president was not just on enactment of legislation but also on enforcement. As part of the program that year, we had workshops on health, education, employment, housing—all issues that are part of day-to-day living.

My Delta Presidency and National Events

In terms of national politics, the four years of my presidency, 1967–71, were divisive and tragic ones for our country. In 1968, for instance, President Johnson's war on poverty was continuing, but we were also fighting in Vietnam, and student protests against the war were taking place. Sometimes major public events occurred, and I felt it was appropriate for me to be at those events in my dual role as commissioner and Delta president.

Delta Sigma Theta event in Chicago. Left to right: Lady Carter, Frankie, Hortense Canady, Dorothy Height, Etta Moten Barnett (artist).

In April 1968, I was in Washington, D.C., for a commission hearing when I heard that Dr. Martin Luther King, Jr., was in Memphis. I remember listening to his speech live on the radio in which he said, "I have been to the mountaintop" and added that we, his people, would get to the promised land, though he might not be with us. I had always admired Dr. King as the eloquent spokesman of the civil rights movement, and he had also been the speaker for a number of programs at my church. The day after this speech I was on my way home in the car when the news broke about his assassination.

Immediately, I contacted Lionel (Loni) and Maxine Newsom in Atlanta and said, "I'm coming to the funeral." The Newsoms were old friends; Shelby and Loni, a well-known educator and former president of Central State University, had been roommates at Lincoln University. They were also both members of Alpha Phi Alpha fraternity, which Dr. King had also belonged to, and Loni was general president of the fraternity. He had arranged for the beautiful Alpha wreath—in the traditional black and gold colors—which was the only floral decoration permitted on Dr. King's grave.

The night before the funeral we went to view the body, and it was a very long line to get into the church. We didn't even think about trying to find a seat for the funeral, though we did go to the cemetery with thousands of others. It was memorable, moving—an opportunity to at least share our grief. Robert Kennedy was also assassinated the following June, and I felt grief and shock then too, but Dr. King was more like family.

After his death, we were all shattered, and some in the black community believed there had been a conspiracy to assassinate this man who was the very symbol of the civil rights struggle. Riots erupted around the country, but St. Louis did not have such violence, and I am not sure exactly why. I was out of town at the time, and I had no personal role in keeping the situation under control here; I am sure the St. Louis black leadership deserves a lot of credit for that. In my own speeches, I have said again and again that it is very easy to let off steam in riots—but you haven't changed the system. What you need to create real change is to become *involved*.

One good thing happened in 1968: the election of William Clay to Congress. For years, I had known him: as an NAACP member, member of the St. Louis Board of Aldermen, a strong supporter of the union movement, an outstanding young St. Louis leader. So when he ran, I voted for him and would have worked on his campaign if my job at the housing authority had allowed me to do so; everything I had a constitutional right to do, I *did*. His election was a breakthrough for the people of Missouri because he brought to Congress a powerful and much-needed voice for black citizens. Among many other things, he helped to found the Congressional Black Caucus (CBC), which I have always supported. In 1971, as Delta president, I authorized the use of the basement of the Delta headquarters in Washington, D.C., by a CBC task force when they were working on a position paper they were preparing to present to the Nixon administration.

Also in 1968, President Johnson decided against seeking reelection and went to live in retirement at his ranch in Texas. I understood why he was not running, but it saddened me; he was my favorite president then, and still is. He had followed through on those positive things that had been started under President Kennedy, and he had a vision for ending

Congressman William Clay.

poverty, ending racial discrimination, and ensuring that all Americans—
black or white—could cast their vote, as the Constitution promised. So
when he announced his decision, I quickly sent a telegram expressing my
sincere admiration for his administration:

> Dear Mr. President, It is difficult for me to express the deep sadness
> I feel because of your announcement that you will not be a
> candidate for reelection. Mr. President, I am sure that I express the
> feelings of millions of Americans in my appeal to you to reconsider
> this position. We are in a time of crisis. No president has faced a
> more difficult challenge on either domestic or foreign issues. No
> other person has your competence to deal with these issues. I pledge
> to you my continued support in your endeavors and I urge you to be
> a candidate for reelection in the 1968 presidential campaign.
>   —Frankie M. Freeman

President Lyndon B. Johnson greets the Deltas.

Two years later, in July 1970, the Delta board of directors was meeting in Houston. Whenever we had a board meeting, we tried to do something for the board. At the recommendation of Lynette Taylor, our executive director, I decided I would find out whether President Johnson was available and take the board to the ranch to visit him. We did just that; we chartered a plane from Houston and went—all twenty or twenty-five of us, as well as two young undergraduates—flying up in the morning and coming back in the afternoon. The plane landed on the ranch somewhere, and we were taken to the president's house. He met with us, took us on a tour, and we talked—just like home folks. It was a high note for all of us, but particularly for the two students who could hardly believe they were in the presence of a former president.

I still treasure something that President Johnson sent me in December 1968: a copy of a speech he had given at Gettysburg on Memorial Day 1963, when he was vice president. The speech, entitled "On this Hallowed Ground," seemed to summarize better than anything else some of the aspirations that he had—and that I admired him for having. It read, in part, "Until justice is blind to color, until education is unaware of race, until opportunity is unconcerned with the color of men's skins, emancipation will be a proclamation but not a fact."

Montgomery Hearings

In December 1958, before I became a member, the Commission on Civil Rights had held its first hearings in Montgomery, Alabama, on the subject of voting rights. The testimony had revealed widespread discrimination against blacks and denial of equal protection—for example, through literacy tests that were used to keep people from registering. In May 1968, we returned to Montgomery for a second round of hearings. The commission would be focusing on economic rights, particularly within the sixteen rural counties in Alabama in which three-fifths of the 362,000 people were black.

As I liked to do, I went down early and visited Bellamy, Alabama, which was a company town for the American Can Company. Other commissioners came with me this time. The song "I owe my soul to the company store" was just a song to us until we actually saw Bellamy and heard the witnesses who came forward.

Two of our first witnesses were Hosea Williams, director of voter registration and political education for the Southern Christian Leadership Conference (SCLC), and Albert Turner, the SCLC's Alabama state director. Mr. Williams gave a strong statement about the background of civil rights activities in Montgomery, from the fight to integrate public accommodations, to the march from Selma to Montgomery. This march, he said, "arous[ed] the conscience of this Nation" and brought together "the forces of good will" which "finally rid us of many of the sick, psychopathic men like some of these county sheriffs...." Mr. Turner then outlined changes that had occurred in Alabama since the march and the passage of the Voting Rights Act of 1965. "Basically," he said, "I think that this bill gave Negroes hope and it gave them a self-pride enough to be able to continue to fight for their other rights." But he added that it also had a negative result since whites, deciding that blacks might now become a political threat, had decided to "economically freeze us out of this area." People were being laid off jobs and forced to leave Alabama and migrate to cities such as Chicago and New York.

We learned why when we heard the next two witnesses, both of them black: John Lee Barnes of York, Alabama, an American Can Company employee for twenty-four years, and Frank Fenderson of Bellamy, an employee for four years. Mr. Fenderson testified that he and his family, including three small children, lived in a three-room company-owned house that had no running water; they shared an outdoor faucet with two other families and had no indoor toilet, only a distant outhouse. He had bought furniture at the company store, plus other supplies, and run up a $300 bill. Every two weeks, when he was paid, the debt came out of his salary. After these deductions, his paycheck usually totaled only $5.

Under questioning by Howard Glickstein, the commission's new staff director, Mr. Fenderson described the racial situation in Bellamy. The restrooms were segregated at the company sawmill where he worked, and so were the churches and swimming pools. Then Mr. Barnes also described the discrimination he had faced in the workplace: that he would train a new white employee, that person would quickly advance to salesman or foreman, and "probably his salary would go to $500 or $650, and mine remained the same thing all the time," he said.

When it was my turn to question the witnesses, I focused on the Bellamy public school, which Mr. Fenderson said was "a Negro school"; the white children in town went to "some kind of training school" by school bus. "I was in Bellamy on Sunday," I said, "and I saw the school. In that school there, in some of the rooms, the panes were out, the only water was one spigot on the outside of the building. The only toilet facilities were about 125 feet away, and it was an outside toilet." Mr. Fenderson said that his own children would have to go there, when they were old enough.

I also asked about the roads, which were covered with gravel in the white section of town—but not in the black section. "Have the Negroes ever asked for gravel on their roads?" I asked. Mr. Barnes replied, "I couldn't say they have, but I know that they would welcome the chance to have gravel. A lot of times the Negro he want things but sometimes he believe that if he asked for it, he won't get it…. We want some of the same things that the whites have."

Finally, Mr. Barnes revealed that a company manager, Hugh C. Sloane, had made an announcement to employees the previous evening, saying that in the future "he might not be able to rent houses, either to colored or white." The reason, said Mr. Barnes, was "the Civil Rights

Commission." That allegation was a potentially damaging one. If it were true, it would constitute a potential violation of the law, which protects witnesses from intimidation.

Mr. Sloane appeared next, under subpoena, accompanied by two company attorneys. They asked that the cameras be cut off and the lights extinguished, and we agreed. Mr. Sloane said that the company owned 168 houses in Bellamy, 45 occupied by whites and 123 by blacks. All of the houses rented by whites had running water and bathrooms, but only 8 of the houses rented by nonwhites had such facilities. At the Bellamy sawmill, he said, there were 340 employees, 270 of them black, but only 2 blacks were assistant supervisors—and they had been promoted during the preceding two weeks. He also admitted that he *had* told employees the company housing situation might change because of the commission hearings.

Our staff director, Bill Taylor, listened to this testimony and voiced the feeling of all of us when he said, after it was over: "I think that most Americans would scarcely believe that such conditions could exist in this country in this century." He requested that the commission formally ask the American Can Company to submit a statement of its plans for dealing with these conditions, within a reasonable time period.

I concurred with that, but I also had a few questions about the company store I had seen in Bellamy. A colleague of Mr. Sloane, Owen Hanson, responded that what the company had attempted to do there "as a convenience for the employee" had been misconstrued as " an exploitation of the employee." He concluded, "Since, however, this has been so sensitive and has had other agencies concerned about it, we've just decided to get out of that business and we're going to notify our employees that effective soon we will not make the payroll deductions at the store, and they can proceed to pay however they wish. And we will give them their checks in the normal course."

A later witness was Dr. Ernest Stone, superintendent of education for the State of Alabama. I asked about the school I had seen in Bellamy, where the only light came from a single bulb in the ceiling, where there was thick red mud outside—even on a dry, sunny day—all the way to the outhouse. I called the conditions "deplorable and disgraceful" and asked what he had to say about this situation. He replied that a number of one-room, one-teacher schools still existed in Alabama, and that they were not only all-black schools. "What you are saying then is that a large number of children, poor black and poor white, are being denied an education, even a decent education of any kind in this state?" I said. He answered, "That is very true."

This is the kind of thing that came out during our hearings. I was outraged by what I heard, and other commissioners felt the same way; you could hear it in some of the questions they asked. Even though this was 1968, fourteen years after the *Brown v. Board of Education* decision, there was still pervasive discrimination—and some blacks just took it for granted or were afraid to say anything about it. At least these hearings brought such things into the open and made them a matter of public record. At each hearing, there were also reporters writing stories that were published across the country. And we asked witnesses, like the ones from American Can Company, about their federal contracts and whether these contracts had non-discrimination clauses. Within a few days of the testimony, our staff would send the appropriate agency a letter, telling them of our findings and asking them to respond.

In this case, there was a positive follow-up to our hearing. Some months later, I got a notice in the mail: the company had closed down the town of Bellamy and instituted a program for community renewal which they called "Cycle to Somewhere."

There was another footnote to this story as well. I mentioned that, throughout our hearings, the staff was always worried about our safety, and particularly *my* safety. One evening, after the Montgomery hearings, I returned to my motel room after dinner. It was a pretty evening in April and I had the curtains open; I could look out—and anyone who wanted to could look in. I was sitting at a table with a member of the Alabama State Advisory Committee, reviewing the day, when boom, something struck the window and broke it. I thought it was a bullet. It apparently was intended for me, but I was not hit.

Soon afterward, a staff member asked what I wanted to do about making the incident public, and I said, "Nothing." The day had been rather tense and emotional, so it could have been someone who was angry about my questions, but I did not want to discuss it. Next day, during the break, a reporter said she had heard that something had happened in my room, but I said there was nothing I had to talk about. Back in St. Louis, I mentioned it to my friend Charlayne Hunter-Gault, who was then a student at Washington University and later became a prominent journalist, and she asked why I had not called the police. I said, "This is Alabama, I just didn't want to do that." I had not been hurt, and I just said, "Leave it alone."

San Antonio Hearing

The commission held another major hearing in December 1968, this time in San Antonio, Texas. We wanted to collect information regarding the civil rights problems of Mexican Americans in Texas, Arizona, California, Colorado, and New Mexico. As a result of our staff investigation, the commission had issued sixty subpoenas to people, including state and federal officials. We had interpreters ready so that witnesses could testify in Spanish; I also had taken Spanish lessons to improve my communication skills.

Our first witnesses, who testified in Spanish, were the nine-member Chavez family of Edcouch, Texas. Their situation was typical of many witnesses: they lived in a four-room house with two bedrooms, and the father, who drove trucks or did farm labor for about $1 an hour, had been able to attend school for only around four years. Overall, we found that among the three major ethnic groups in Texas, the Mexican American population had the least formal education, which meant that their unemployment rate was high and their income comparatively low.

One interesting aspect of this hearing for me was the fact that I chaired the last two sessions, after Chairman Hannah and Commissioner Hesburgh had to leave early. The first focused on employment practices at Kelly Air Force Base in Texas. A Trinity College professor had conducted a study showing that minorities employed at Kelly from 1917 to 1966 did not have equal opportunity. Witnesses from the Air Force followed and promised that they would take corrective action. In the final session, we dealt with administration of justice issues, including a complaint of police brutality against a Texas highway patrolman who had assaulted three people. He did not deny the charges—but the district attorney had not sought any indictments. In closing this hearing, I said the following:

> It is imperative that all of us understand the problems and frustrations of those whose native towns and customs might differ from ours. America can ill afford to permit the oppression of a people simply because their language and culture are different from ours. All of our nation's groups must be listened to whether we agree with their views or not. They should be afforded all possible opportunities to succeed in work, school, and business.... I now ask your indulgence as I attempt the following:

> Nos ha dado mucho placer de venir a San Antonio. Esperamos que etas audiencias sena effectivas y para el beneficio de todo el Pueblo Mexico Americano. Sigan en la lucha para obtener sus derechos civiles porque de lo que hacemos en estos dias depende el future de nuestros hijos.

> [We have been pleased to come to San Antonio. We hope that these hearings are effective and for the benefit of the whole Mexican American community. Continue in your struggle to obtain your civil rights because the future of our children depends on our actions during these days.]

Back Home

During these years, many things were happening in my personal life as well. In 1966, Shelby and I moved to a fourteen-room house on Waterman Place in the Central West End; we were the first black family on our block. Our house had a big back yard where we did a lot of entertaining—barbecues mostly—in the summer. Later my husband decided that he wanted a pool, so in 1974 we put one in. Shelby was still an employee of the Department of Defense and active in the community, particularly with Junior Achievement. Pat had graduated from Sumner High School and gone on to Grinnell College in Iowa. In

Pat with husband, Ellis Bullock, Jr., 1977.

1960, she got married, but the marriage ended a short time later; subsequently, she finished her undergraduate degree at Washington University, where she concentrated on dance. Afterward, she worked for the Urban League and then moved to New York City and worked for the YWCA. After studying for a master's degree in theater and dance at Mount Holyoke College, she became grants administrator for the Bronx Council on the Arts and then the director of the dance programs for the New York State Council for the Arts.

In 1975, she met Ellis Bullock, Jr., a widower with three young sons. Several months later, she called her daddy and said she was thinking about getting married. Shelby said, "Doesn't he have some children?" And she replied, "Yes, three boys. Don't you want some grandchildren? Because that is how you are going to get them!" They were married in May 1976. The youngest, Darren, spent summers with us. When he and Shelby went out, Shelby would tell folks, "This is my grandson," and they would say, "Well, he looks just like you."

On the job, I was still associate general counsel for the land clearance and housing authority, handling housing authority business primarily, while Irv Dagen, the general counsel, took care of land clearance authority matters. My job involved a variety of things: preparing and reviewing contracts and other documents; representing the authority in court and at legislative hearings; pressing nonpayment of rent cases, termination of lease agreements, and so on—for the 164 buildings and nearly 6,900 units that the housing authority was overseeing at that time. Our housing projects included Carr Square Village, Clinton Peabody Terrace, Cochran Garden Apartments, George L. Vaughn Apartments, Vaughn Senior Citizens Building, Joseph M. Darst Apartments, and A. M. Webbe Apartments.

Most problematic of all were the Captain Wendell O. Pruitt Homes and the William L. Igoe Apartments, known collectively as Pruitt-Igoe. They were side-by-side developments of eleven-story apartment buildings: Pruitt, which had been completed in September 1955, had twenty buildings with a total of 1,736 units; Igoe, finished in May 1956, had thirteen buildings with 1,134 units. The architects and government officials had made decisions that created serious problems. For example, the elevators stopped only on every other floor, and there was no place where children could play.

At the end of 1968, trouble arose when the housing authority decided to raise rents across the board in the housing projects under its control. This decision was bitterly controversial: the housing authority felt that the cost of its operations had increased, so the increase was justified, but the tenants complained that necessary repairs had not been made to their apartments. Led by Jean King and the Reverend Buck Jones, and advised by Legal Aid Society lawyers including Richard Baron, the tenants initiated a rent strike. Starting in February 1969, they refused to pay rent and made a number of demands: that rents be geared to tenants' ability to pay, and no more than 25 percent of the income of public-assistance tenants; that tenants be included on the housing authority board; that living conditions improve; and that a moratorium be instituted on all lawsuits and evictions in connection with the strike.

During the period of the strike, we had to initiate more than five hundred suits for non-payment of rent. When the cases came up for trial, we obtained judgment for the amount of delinquent rent, but we took no steps to evict the tenants. The rent that tenants did pay was placed in escrow until the strike was settled.

Behind the scenes, I offered recommendations on what should be done to end the strike. I suggested solving a pressing need for larger apartments, suitable for families with children, by combining vacant one-bedroom units to create larger spaces; I also recommended creating additional buildings solely for the elderly. At Pruitt-Igoe, I said, all tenants should have a greater leadership voice, a demonstration school should be established for residents' vocational education, and tenant "sweat equity" should also be counted toward the new rent schedule. I had conversations with the Labor Department to fund elevator repair and maintenance training programs.

For a long time, I had recognized that having the elevators stop on every other floor was a serious design problem, and I had talked repeatedly with management about that. I had heard these and other tenant complaints in my meetings with them over the years, and, although I was an employee of the housing authority, I think they knew I was in sympathy with some of their demands. It was an awkward situation for me, but anyone who has worked for the government, or a university or a company, has at some time been in a situation like that. And I also felt there was right on the authority's side; in my meetings with tenant groups, I always said they had to take responsibility for caring for the building, curbing vandalism, and maintaining their property.

Nine months later the strike was finally settled, with some concessions to the strikers, particularly the 25 percent rent-increase limit and a new tenant participation structure. As part of the settlement, the federal government mandated that the agency operate as two separate corporations: the St. Louis Housing Authority, which would focus on low-income housing, and the Land Clearance and Redevelopment Authority, focusing on land clearance and redevelopment. At the same time, Irv Dagen became general counsel of the land clearance authority, and in August 1969, I became general counsel of the housing authority. My responsibility was to supervise the legal department and interpret the rights and obligations of the agency under local, state, and federal laws.

McDonnell Douglas—and Dramatic Results

All this time, I was still using my leave time to travel to Washington, D.C., for meetings of the Civil Rights Commission. We were getting ready for new hearings in January 1970—the commission's seventeenth since its founding—and this time they would be held in St. Louis County. We wanted to examine the racial implications of suburban development in relation to minority housing and employment. As an example, we decided to look at the employment policies of Mallinckrodt Chemical Works, Chrysler Corporation, and McDonnell Douglas Corporation, the fourth-largest defense contractor in the United States and the largest employer in the St. Louis metropolitan area, with 33,007 employees at the time of our hearing.

As government contractors, these companies all had to comply with Executive Order 11246, which required companies with federal contracts to have affirmative-action programs for equal employment opportunity. But we heard testimony at the hearing that in December 1969, the federal government had awarded McDonnell Douglas a $7.7 billion contract for F-15 fighter jets—a great boon to the company and to the local economy—without a review of the affirmative-action plan that McDonnell Douglas had recently submitted to comply with 11246. Furthermore, an earlier plan they had in place at that time was completely inadequate. The commissioners decided to write to Defense Secretary Melvin Laird outlining these facts and asking that corrective action be taken promptly. In turn, the Department of Defense admitted that it had made a mistake and took remedial action, notifying McDonnell Douglas that their contract was suspended pending an approved affirmative-action plan.

Immediately, there was a tremendous public furor. On February 4, 1970, the *St. Louis Globe-Democrat* wrote an editorial entitled "Tea-Pot Tempest," in which they defended McDonnell Douglas's record in the area of non-discrimination in employment. They mentioned the company's hiring of six thousand blacks during the mid-1960s for aircraft manufacturing jobs as part of the F-4 Phantom project. They also defended the recent dismissal of black workers as part of a general layoff made necessary by the cancellation of two major contracts and described Percy Green, who had brought suit against the company in an attempt to force them to rehire him, as "a compulsive troublemaker."

As a member of the Civil Rights Commission, I wrote a reply to this editorial on February 6, which was published in the paper. I said that I too wanted the matter to be resolved quickly, but I did not believe that it

> should be dismissed, as you have done, as a "teapot tempest." Equal employment opportunity has grave implications not only for St. Louis but for the rest of the country. At stake is the principle that all Americans should have the same opportunity for jobs and promotions. Unless there is this equality of opportunity, we will continue to hurtle toward two separate societies.

The U.S. Commission on Civil Rights , ca. 1970. Left to right: front row—Theodore Hesburgh, John Hannah, Robert Rankin; back row—Hector Garcia, Howard Glickstein, Frankie, Maurice Mitchell.

I went on to say that, during our January hearings, Claude Crowl, chief of the Department of Defense Contract Compliance Office for the St. Louis area, had told us that the latest McDonnell Douglas plan was "inadequate in that it did not contain the 'specific goals and timetables' requested by the Department of Defense." Without an acceptable plan that contained all these elements, I said, "all the rhetoric about equal opportunity is meaningless." I added that testimony at our hearing from company officials had left the commissioners with "the conviction that there is a lack of understanding and commitment to equal employment opportunity" on their part.

Further, I added, the company's record of affirmative action over the past twenty years had been far from stellar; in fact, "blacks have progressed at a snail-like pace." While blacks represented less than 1 percent of the company's officers and managers, and less than 1 percent of all professionals, they made up 39.4 percent of service workers and 72.5 percent of laborers. "As a St. Louisan," I said, "I am aware of the tremendous importance of the McDonnell Douglas Corporation in the economic life of this area, but I also believe the company has an obligation to provide meaningful implementation of its announced commitment to equal employment opportunity."

On the day that this response appeared, I received a surprise letter from the St. Louis Housing Authority, signed by the board chairman, Clarence Swarm, and the four board members, Frank Boykin, Thelma Green, Reverend Carl Dudley, and Reverend Donald Register. "It is with grave reluctance that we must advise you that your services with the Authority will be terminated as of February 6, 1970, at the close of the business day." The company was angry, the community was angry; I was regarded as a troublemaker by McDonnell Douglas and the *Globe-Democrat*—and they did not need a troublemaker on the housing authority staff. I had seen this kind of thing done before but never in such a bold, daring way. Ironically, McDonnell Douglas was only without their contract for ten days or so. They got themselves together, complied, and developed an acceptable affirmative-action plan with the appropriate goals and timetables. The government approved it, and the contract was back on track.

Meanwhile, I was supposed to be out of my office by 5:00 that same day, but I actually had everything cleared out by 2:30. I was angry and hurt, of course, but I did not talk to the reporters who called me. I did call the NAACP and other people that I knew; they called other folks, and pretty soon the whole town knew. The civil rights enforcement people phoned and asked whether I wanted to file a complaint, and I said no. I felt that the housing authority had a right to choose its attorney, and if they did not want me to represent them, then I would not represent them.

However, others spoke up for me. Joseph Clark, who was president of the St. Louis chapter of the NAACP, charged publicly that I had been fired because of my role in the St. Louis hearings. The housing authority, of course, denied this accusation. They said my dismissal had to do with a need to cut expenses.

I had immediately notified the Civil Rights Commission, and on February 11, the staff director, Howard Glickstein, wrote a letter of complaint to George W. Romney, secretary of Housing and Urban Development (HUD). A week later, Assistant Secretary Cox replied, saying that HUD would investigate. On March 11, the commission's director wrote again, "expressing the commission's hope that in view of Mrs. Freeman's national stature and her position as a presidentially appointed member of the commission, the investigation would be conducted speedily." Mr. Cox again replied that the inquiry was proceeding but that a reply would not come for several weeks.

On March 31, the commission still had not received any reply, and Father Theodore M. Hesburgh—by then the chairman—wrote an angry letter to Secretary Romney, in which he said that the commission was concerned about "reports in some of the St. Louis newspapers that [Mrs. Freeman's dismissal] was linked to her participation as a member of this Commission in the hearings held in St. Louis last January." In addition, he said, "to date the only responses the Commission has received to its expressions of concern and requests for information have been two uninformative letters from Assistant Secretary Cox, in one of which Mrs. Freeman's name was not even spelled correctly." He asked for Secretary Romney's personal attention to this matter.

But I did not file a complaint, nor did I want anyone to file a complaint on my behalf. I knew that, even if they offered me the job again, I did not want to go back there. I wanted to get myself together and move on.

A few days afterward, when it actually hit me that I was no longer employed, I decided to do something for myself. I had never had a full-length fur coat, so I went down to Stix, Baer & Fuller's fur department and told them I wanted to have a mink coat made—the best available. Then the man asked about arrangements for payment and I told him I would put it on my charge card, which was in my husband's name. When I got home, I told Shelby; he was a person who would never have put *anything* like this on his charge—but he understood. He did say, "Frankie, how are you going to pay for this?" And I said, "Don't worry. I'm going back into private practice."

I took a few days off to visit friends in Florida, but after that I needed to find an office. In addition to his position with the federal government, Shelby was also the owner of a property management company called Sphinx Management, located on Hodiamont Avenue. I rented some extra space in that building, had some stationery made up, and hired a secretary. I was back in the practice of law again.

About two months after my termination, I got a phone call from Robert Hyland of KMOX radio offering me a part-time job as a community consultant with the station. I was paid a small monthly stipend and received some CBS stock for a couple of years. I never knew for sure, but I thought that some of my friends had probably talked to him and that Mr. Hyland saw this position as a way of offsetting what had happened to me. It was a small but stable income while I built up my law practice.

I also remember a public event from that period at which I was present with people from McDonnell Douglas and there was definitely a little chill in the air—but it did pass after a while. And, as my brother Andy told me, fourteen years was too long to be on one job anyway. It was time to be back in private practice.

Chapter Seven

My Last Years on the Commission

1972–78

FROM MY NEW OFFICE, I spent the next year getting reestablished in the general practice of law, taking a mix of cases: divorces, wills, estates, probate matters, and so on. Then a new opportunity came my way and for a little over a year I joined two attorneys, Forrest Elliot and Murray Marks, in their law firm—renamed Elliot, Marks, and Freeman—located on Delmar close to Hamilton. When Elliot, who was the managing partner, chose to dissolve the firm, I once again needed an office of my own, and this time I decided that I wanted to be closer to the downtown courts. So in 1974, I moved east to the old Beaumont Medical Building at 3720 Washington. After about two years there, I was invited by Harold Whitfield and Rita Montgomery to join their firm in the Paul Brown Building at 818 Olive Street. We called our new partnership Freeman, Whitfield, Montgomery, and Walton.

Throughout this period, I handled occasional civil rights cases, though I no longer focused on them. One of the most memorable was the case of Edward Haynie, the only black student admitted to the first class in the new School of Dental Medicine at Southern Illinois University at Edwardsville (SIUE). Two years later, he became the only student dismissed from his class before graduating. In newspaper articles, Haynie described his tenure at the school as "psychological hell," saying that he had been subjected to discriminatory acts by faculty and that students and school officials failed to provide the support he needed, including the same kind of financial assistance that white students had received. He also said he was the only student in his class asked to submit to psychological testing.

Haynie asked me to represent him, so I contacted the national NAACP, which assigned Charles E. Carter from New York City to work with me as co-counsel. In August 1978, I filed a discrimination suit against SIUE in U.S. District Court for the Southern District of Illinois; it was based on Title VI of the Civil Rights Act of 1964, which required agencies that are recipients of federal funds to use those funds without discrimination. While the university denied that discrimination was involved in Haynie's dismissal, the NAACP saw his case as part of its ongoing battle to force professional schools to admit blacks and retain them once they were admitted. Furthermore, since only one black had graduated from the dental program in the first six years of its existence, we believed that the problem went far beyond Haynie himself. So we put SIUE on notice that we might turn the case into a class-action suit.

After we had taken all the depositions, the defendants settled the case, agreeing that Haynie would be readmitted. However, he decided not to go back to dental school. Instead, he continued his education at the University of Florida and received a Ph.D. in chemistry. After that, he taught at Harris-Stowe State College and at the University of Missouri–St. Louis. In the late 1990s, he received a Lifetime Achievement Award from the St. Louis County branch of the NAACP.

I did not feel that it was unusual for him to decide not to attend the dental program, even after his suit had succeeded. Over the years, a number of my clients have done something similar. In fact, I often tell clients when they come in for an initial consultation on a civil rights matter that even if they win their case, they may find the climate will not be a good one for them to remain in their old job, school, or position. People may see them as troublemakers or they may feel so bitter them-selves that they will not wish to continue. But at the same time, I say to them, it will make a difference to others if they can hold out. I under-stand that the dental school at SIUE, for example, now has many black students and graduates—so Haynie was a kind of trailblazer, paving the way for all of them.

Frankie in her law office, ca. 1978.

During these years, I also handled a civil rights matter for Celestine Hawkins, who had been a principal in the St. Louis Public Schools, moving up from an elementary school to a middle school. She thought she was eligible for a high-school position but was denied promotion. Although she was African American, she was not turned down on that basis; in fact, the supervisor who made the decision was also African American. The refusal was based on her gender; she was told that the job had to be given to a man. So I represented her, filing suit in St. Louis federal court against the St. Louis Board of Education on the basis of Title IX of the Civil Rights Act of 1964, which prohibited discrimination based on gender. This time, we did not even finish the depositions before the board agreed to resolve the case in her favor. A little while later, I ran into an attorney from the law firm that represented the board, and he said, "Frankie, the *next* time you have a problem on this kind of issue, call me before filing suit!"

At that time, I believed—and still believe today—that achieving women's rights is essential to achieving racial justice. All human inequality based on factors such as race, gender, religion, and national origin is simply wrong; you cannot rail against one and ignore or condone the others. And, as a practical matter, 50 percent of all minorities are women and, therefore, in double jeopardy. If we were suddenly able to eliminate all racial inequality in the United States, minority women would *still* face restricted choices by virtue of their gender. The challenge, I think, is to achieve equality for minority men and women of all races, who together represent the majority of this country's population.

Commission Reports and Repercussions

Throughout this period, the Civil Rights Commission was still holding hearings and preparing reports. In March 1970, we released a study, "Racism in America and How to Combat It," the first we had published on this subject. It was done by Anthony Downs, a senior vice president of the Real Estate Research Corporation and consultant to the RAND Corporation, who talked about the significance of racism, which he defined as "any attitude, action, or institutional structure which subordinates a person or group because of fears of their color."

I have always talked in similar terms to groups about racism. To move away from racism, I feel we need to get to know one another. I ask the organization I am addressing, whether it is white or black: "If you found yourself in an emergency, whom would you call? Would any of the ten friends you called be a person of another color?" While some people see continuing racism among our young people, I personally see a generational shift in the answer to this question. While people my age would probably know only one or two people of another color, my grandson's best friend might well be a person of another color. That is where the hope lies today.

The commission went on to publish other crucial reports. Since the St. Louis hearing in 1970 had highlighted the fact that the federal government, through its various agencies, was not always enforcing its own civil rights laws, we decided to investigate this whole issue further and soon released a report, "Federal Civil Rights Enforcement Effort." Because the president has ultimate responsibility for overseeing this effort, we decided to begin with the White House, then go on to about forty federal agencies. Overall, we found that the government's civil rights enforcement effort was inadequate. Only one department—Health, Education, and Welfare (HEW)—got a "fair" score, while all the others rated "poor."

Every contract issued by these agencies requires non-discrimination on the basis of race, creed, color, gender, nationality, etc., but we found that these agencies were often not enforcing this stipulation. They had good quality control in other areas; that is, if Housing and Urban Development (HUD) wrote a contract about housing, they would look closely at the proposed architectural plan. They just did not take the same care in overseeing the equal employment opportunity provision. So we recommended that they increase their staff in this area or give staff members the authority they needed. And one department that did make major changes to its compliance procedures was the Department of Defense. In 1971, it began insisting that its more than thirty-five contractors develop strong equal opportunity programs. In some cases, it even issued "show cause" notices, a step that can lead to imposition of sanctions.

We also criticized the U.S. Equal Employment Opportunity Commission (EEOC), an agency created in 1964 to end employment discrimination and to promote programs that would make equal employment opportunity a reality. The EEOC, we said, "has been adversely affected by a rapid turnover and long vacancies in key agency positions such as chairman, commission members, executive director, general counsel, and director of compliance."

Before we released this report to the public, however, we sent our findings to the departments we mentioned. If they thought we had made mistakes, and could prove it, we changed our report; if they could not, we included what they said, but we also included our rebuttal. At the same time, we sent the report to President Richard Nixon's lawyer, Leonard Garment, and he was upset by it. He wanted us to delay its release until after the midterm elections in November, but we did not do so; instead, we publicized the contents of the report at a news conference.

By that time, the composition of the commission had changed. In October 1967, Erwin Griswold had resigned to become solicitor general of the United States, a position he held until 1973. Eugene C. Patterson, who had been appointed with me, resigned in September 1968 to become the executive managing editor of the *St. Petersburg Times*. John Hannah, who was chairman when I first became a member, had resigned in February 1969 to become the administrator of the U.S. Agency for International Development (USAID), which administers economic assistance programs for developing countries.

In their places, we had new members: Maurice B. Mitchell, chancellor of the University of Denver, appointed in September 1968; Hector P. Garcia, a physician from Corpus Christi, Texas, named in November 1968, though he stayed only a year; Stephen Horn, who was then from American University but soon became president of California State University at Long Beach, appointed in December 1969; and Manuel Ruiz, Jr., an attorney from Los Angeles, appointed in January 1970. By the early 1970s, the only two commissioners still left from the time of my appointment were Robert S. Rankin, who had been appointed in 1960, and Father Hesburgh, who had become chairman in March 1969.

After John Hannah left, I mentioned to him that I would be very interested in a short-term USAID assignment—and he notified me in 1971 that I had been named one of two delegates to a United Nations Economic Commission for Africa (UNECA) conference on housing in Lome, Togo, West Africa; the other delegate was Samuel C. Jackson, assistant secretary for community planning and management in the Department of Housing and Urban Development. At the conference, I would make presentations on housing in the U.S. and afterward visit seven other countries—Ghana, Ivory Coast, Ethiopia, Kenya, Tunisia, Senegal, Liberia—where USAID either had, or was planning to have, housing guaranty programs. In all, I would be gone for six weeks.

It was an opportunity of a lifetime for me. First I flew to Washington for a briefing, then on to New York, London, and finally Africa. The plane stopped in the Ivory Coast en route to Togo, and I just had to get off briefly. This was my first visit to Africa and I felt so emotional about going back to the motherland that I had to set foot on African soil at the earliest moment possible, then we flew on to Togo and the conference. I was well prepared for it; as the federal government always does, USAID had sent me a huge stack of reading materials. But I was surprised to go back to my pleasant, government-owned hotel after the first day at the conference—only to find that there was no water! When I inquired, I discovered that you could only get water for three or four hours each day, and you never knew when it would be shut off. People there were accustomed to this situation and kept a bucket in the bathroom that they filled whenever water was available. My first postcard home to Shelby read: "Having a great time, but there is no water. I can't even flush the toilet!"

After the weeklong conference, I was to tour around, meeting with local officials. As a representative of the U.S. government, I had translators available to me, which made the whole experience so much more meaningful. Before I left St. Louis, friends had warned me, "Now be sure that you don't stick with just the official people." So wherever I went, I looked for opportunities to meet with ordinary people in markets, homes, and elsewhere and talk with them about their concerns.

I also visited family along the way. In Liberia, I had one cousin, Wilma Holland; she was married to a Liberian, Harry Morris, whom she had met in Danville, and he owned the largest rubber plantation in the country. Another cousin, Helene Holland, was also married to a Liberian, Frank Roberts, who was related to President William V. S. Tubman. While I was in Monrovia, I stayed in the residence of old friends, the American ambassador, Dr. Samuel Z. Westerfield, and his wife Helene, a fellow Delta member.

In Kenya, I also had the chance to see Muthoni and Peter again. They had an apartment in Nairobi then, and they showed me the sights, taking me to a game preserve where we saw elephants and zebras and to the village to meet their parents. On this trip, I also began my collection, which grew on later visits, of African art, masks, and artifacts.

Violence at a Hearing

On February 14, 1972, the Civil Rights Commission began a hearing that we said was the "first major effort by a federal agency to investigate denial of equal opportunity to Puerto Ricans in the New York metropolitan area." In preceding months, state advisory committees in

Massachusetts, Connecticut, New Jersey, and New York had held fact-finding meetings on this subject, and our staff had gathered information through more than one thousand community interviews. Now we were planning a four-day hearing in New York City to highlight problems in four areas: education, public housing, employment opportunity, and administration of justice.

That Monday, Father Hesburgh had to adjourn the hearing early because members of two dissident Puerto Rican groups interrupted a session on job opportunities. Then in the Tuesday morning session, we were startled to hear several people, members of the Puerto Rican Socialist Party, suddenly begin shouting "Stop the farce" and waving placards that called for Puerto Rican independence. This demonstration disrupted the hearing for about an hour, but eventually the group quieted down and left the room, though two were arrested. One was later quoted in a Washington newspaper as saying, "These commissions never accomplish anything; they are part of the establishment."

Late on the afternoon of the second day, just as we were hearing testimony from two city high-school principals, we were surprised to hear someone shout, "We want Puerto Ricans to speak for us, not whites, blacks, or anyone else." Men dressed in military-style garb began shouting and scuffling. Father Hesburgh banged his gavel for quiet, but several people ran up to the podium, grabbed our microphones, and began singing the Puerto Rican anthem. One man pulled a news photographer from a raised platform at the rear of the room and threw him to the ground. Later we found out that these were members of four dissident Puerto Rican groups.

Immediately, federal marshals began trying to seize the ringleaders and restore order in the hall, but a man threw a chair at them. When the melee was over, the marshals had arrested four people. I was stunned by all of this; it was the only time in the history of the commission, and in my own experience, when there had ever been such violence. My first reaction was to get under the table. Then, when it was clear that order would not be restored, Father Hesburgh told the marshals to remove us, so we quickly left the podium through a curtain at the rear of the stage. I remember being frightened and thinking, "I must get out of here. I *must* get out of here."

As usual, this hearing was being televised, so this disruption was broadcast around the nation. In fact, Father Hesburgh alluded to this in a newspaper article afterward: "They don't give a hoot about building an objective record of the problems; they want to be on the tube," he said.

We were all frustrated by what had happened. Most of the demonstrators wanted to talk about Puerto Rican independence—and the Civil Rights Commission was the *wrong* venue for that discussion. Our role was to investigate and make public the problems of Puerto Ricans who had come to the United States, and in this way we could identify the need for new legislation or better enforcement of existing laws.

So the six of us met to decide what to do next. We all reluctantly decided that because of two telephoned bomb threats and threats that had been made to witnesses—some of whom were now afraid to testify—the hearings would have to be halted. We would collect the statements of all the witnesses who had not been able to speak and publish them in a book, along with the hearing transcript.

Before the hearing, we had also asked Piri Thomas, a Puerto Rican American author, to attend the hearings and write an account of what he heard, and we published it in a special edition of the *Civil Rights Digest*. It was not intended to cover everything that happened—and, in fact, it did not reflect the view of the commissioners or the staff. Still, he did describe the roots of the violence graphically as "an ugly head of despair, frustration, exploitation, hot-and-cold running cockroaches, king-sized rats, crummy tenement slum houses, poor education, and mucho job discrimination." What he said about the frustration and the hostility of the Puerto Rican community struck home with me. Some people in the black community also felt there was no way out, no way to *make* it, except through crime and drugs. So it was ironic when I heard the demonstrators say, "No black can speak for us." They were talking about me.

In the end, the disruption was such a waste. After the demonstrators finished and the hearing was called off—after everyone had gone home—all those problems in education, housing, and jobs that had been there to begin with, were all still there. Nothing had changed. But at least we had tried, and that is a positive thing.

Cairo Hearings

Days after President Nixon was reelected in November 1972, Father Hesburgh received a phone call from the White House: he was being asked to resign from the commission because of long-standing differences with the administration. His replacement as chairman, named in 1974, was another fine man, Arthur S. Flemming, an educator who had served as president of three colleges and universities. Dr. Flemming, a Republican who had been secretary of health, education, and welfare under President Dwight D. Eisenhower, was also a strong civil rights advocate. As sorry as I was to see Father Hesburgh leave, I was pleased with Dr. Flemming's appointment.

The commission continued its work with a 1972 subcommittee hearing in Cairo, Illinois, which I chaired; the other commissioner present was Maurice Mitchell. As I said in my opening statement, the commission had decided to come to Cairo because of reports that extensive, overt racial discrimination existed there and that government officials at all levels had failed to enforce civil rights laws. We wanted to determine whether those allegations were true and, if they were, what could be done to resolve such problems in Cairo and other communities troubled by poverty, racial strife, and apathetic government officials.

After two and a half days of testimony, we felt that we had seen the contrast between what was and what might have been. Every time officials tried to explain why something had not happened, they had to admit they had not done all they could. The result was that little progress had been made toward equal rights for all. For example, the public schools had been integrated, but a new private school remained all white despite its assurances that blacks were not excluded. A nonprofit housing corporation and a government-sponsored clinic had biracial boards, yet municipal commissions and public bodies were still all white.

Housing was a key problem area. The city government had thwarted the board of the housing corporation in its efforts to provide low- and moderate-income housing—even though half the people of Cairo were then living in substandard housing. In a clear violation of federal guidelines, public housing in Cairo was almost totally segregated, and the housing authority's executive director had testified that he would not integrate this housing because he feared racial hostility. But that was not all. There was a shortage of health-care programs, and white dentists were refusing to treat black patients. Unemployment was a general problem, especially for black residents who, even when they did find a job, were often refused promotion. Overall, there was an atmosphere of deep despair. Half the citizens had left in recent years, especially young people, and one-third of those remaining received public assistance.

In our report, we made a number of recommendations in the areas of education, housing, health, employment, and administration of justice. I personally met with the Illinois governor, Richard Ogilvie, to explain the commission's findings and ask for his help in solving these problems. In an open letter to the people of Cairo, which was published in the local newspaper, the commission called upon them to help "end the madness." It was, we said, making that city "a prison for every one of its citizens."

In 1973, the commission returned briefly to Cairo for a follow-up visit and found that little had changed. But slowly, gradually, there *was* progress. In 1980, a federal court ordered a change in the way that city council members were elected, saying that the previous system—which had resulted in an all-white council, despite a large black population in Cairo—was discriminatory. Now the council members would have to be elected by district, not "at large" as before. And in 1983, the first three black members were elected to the city council.

Even more significant, the racial climate seemed to change. In 1992, for example, an all-white jury convicted a white Cairo police officer in the 1991 killing of a black man who had been shot fourteen times in the back. This kind of conviction could not have taken place just a few years earlier. And Preston Ewing, a black citizen of Cairo and president of the local NAACP chapter who testified before us in 1972, became city treasurer. All these things show that a community can make progress, even though the struggle continues.

Later Hearings

Throughout the next six years, the commission underwent still more changes. Maurice Mitchell left in 1974, and the following January, Rabbi Murray Saltzman was named to the commission. By that point, Robert Rankin and I had served for the longest time of any of the commissioners.

Although many of our hearings had focused on the problems of blacks, our charter urged us to hear any citizens who were deprived of their rights because of race, color, religion, gender, or national origin. In October 1973, we embarked on a four-day hearing in Window Rock, Arizona, at the Navajo Nation. A year earlier, we had laid the groundwork for this effort by holding Native American hearings in Albuquerque and Phoenix, and the testimony we heard then had revealed some shocking statistics: an Indian unemployment rate eight to thirteen times greater than the overall rates for New Mexico and Arizona, an average educational level far below that of the general population, a relatively high infant mortality rate, and a short life expectancy.

Frankie (middle) with Commissioners Manuel Ruiz, Jr., Rabbi Murray Saltzman, Arthur Flemming (chair), and Stephen Horn at a U.S. Commission on Civil Rights hearing, 1976.

Frankie (on the right side of the table, second from far end) at a U.S. Commission on Civil Rights meeting at the White House with President Carter, July 8, 1977.

In this hearing we explored these issues, as well as areas of economic potential for the Navajo, who were routinely exploited by others. As I said in a statement at the close of the hearing, "The Navajo Reservation is rich in mineral resources, but the area has been virtually colonized by outside developers. Strip-mining is now conducted under long-term leases that fail to mention the method of coal extraction, do not guarantee restoration of the land, and make no provision for sharing profits." Later we found similar problems with the Sioux tribe in South Dakota. In 1977, we also held hearings in Seattle on the American Indian tribes of the Northwest, but these focused mainly on conflicts between Indians and non-Indians over fishing rights and government jurisdiction.

Then in 1976, we held hearings on gender and racial discrimination on television and afterward moved on to consider age discrimination, issuing a report in which we found that it existed in the delivery of federally supported services and benefits within each of the federal programs we examined. We also issued several studies of affirmative action and how it can be used to assure equal opportunity for all. Then, in a 1978 report on "Social Indicators of Equality for Minorities and Women," we found serious and continuing problems of inequality in education, earnings, and housing.

Reflecting on the Commission

Although I did not know it at the time, my own tenure on the U.S. Commission on Civil Rights was drawing to a close. The commission was continuing to find evidence of discrimination and disparate treatment—which were often occurring because officials had failed to enforce existing laws or because government agencies insisted that they did not have any civil rights responsibility. Some people made excuses for such treatment and opposed us when we supported affirmative action as a remedy.

But I do not want to sound negative because throughout all of this work, through all the commission hearings and reports to the various presidents, we did make progress. Of course, we still have problems as a society, but there has been substantial improvement in the three basic areas—denial of equal housing, denial of education, denial of equal employment opportunities—important themes in many of our hearings, whether they were in Mississippi or Massachusetts, New Mexico or Missouri.

I think we made a difference as a commission by exposing these problems in a credible way, through extensive fact-finding and thorough reports. In each case, we also made specific recommendations for change a part of our reports to the president and Congress—and they have been referred to in Supreme Court decisions and in subsequent legislation. As I have mentioned, some provisions of the Voting Rights Act of 1965 were recommended by the commission.

For me, this period in my life was an opportunity for public service and a chance to pursue issues related to public policy. It was also an exciting time; I had access to information that, as a private citizen, I probably would not have had. Mainly, though, I have always wanted to be of service and to make a difference: that's what I pray for and that's how I want to live. My work with the commission gave me that chance.

Chapter Eight

Inspector General—Briefly

1979–81

IT WAS 1979, AND JIMMY CARTER WAS PRESIDENT. That March I was attending a Civil Rights Commission meeting in Baltimore when I got a message that the White House was trying to reach me. They said they wanted me to come over and meet with someone on the domestic-policy staff about a presidential appointment. Of course, I followed up right away and found out that I was being considered for the position of inspector general in either of two agencies: the Environmental Protection Agency (EPA) or the Community Services Administration (CSA), the federal anti-poverty agency. During our conversation, the White House staff member told me, "I think you would fit best with the CSA." Later on, it turned out that the only *other* female inspector general was appointed to the EPA.

Immediately, I began to wonder, "Where did *that* come from?" I did not have any idea who had recommended me. My first thought was Missouri senator Thomas Eagleton; I knew him and his family well. Years earlier, I had been on the campaign committee for his father, Mark Eagleton, when he ran against Raymond Tucker in the Democratic primary for mayor of St. Louis. When I got back home, I called Senator Eagleton to inquire—but he did not know anything about it, though he said he would actively support my confirmation. I never actually found out for sure who did suggest my name, though I now believe it was again Louis Martin. It had to have come from a political figure or from someone high up in the Democratic Party, and Louis Martin, who had previously recommended me for the commission, fit that description.

At the time, I knew a little about the office, but I quickly got a copy of the law and gathered more information. Senator Eagleton was the Senate sponsor of the Inspector General Act of 1978, which had created the position of inspector general in twelve government departments, including the CSA. The inspectors general were intended to be independent overseers who would address problems of waste, fraud, abuse, mismanagement, and inefficiency in federal departments and agencies. All the auditing and investigative responsibilities for each agency would be consolidated under the inspector general, who would work to improve the efficiency and effectiveness of government operations. In three other agencies, inspectors general were already on board, so altogether there would be fifteen in place.

The law had been enacted in the wake of the Billie Sol Estes scandal of 1962, when he was convicted of mail fraud and conspiracy to defraud the government. Before that time, every agency had auditing and investigative staffs to monitor their own activities. But when those staff members found a problem, they had to go through channels to report it, and their supervisor had to decide whether it was valid or not. Of course, that meant many problems were swept under the rug. As a result, Congress and the public pushed for the inspector-general law, signed by President Carter on October 12, 1978, which provided for an independent officer who would report to Congress.

As the act specified, the government was looking for appointees who had extensive investigative and auditing experience, good character, and a strong personality—all important since the person selected had to aggressively investigate allegations of wrongdoing. In the CSA, for example, an Administration Inspection Division already existed, but its chief had testified before a congressional committee that he had been denied permission to investigate a number of such allegations. One such case had later resulted in twenty-two indictments.

This position sounded very interesting to me, and it would be a great honor, but it would also require me to live in Washington, D.C. So before I did anything about it, I went home and talked it over with Shelby. We decided that we could manage it: I would take an apartment there and get back home as often as possible; he would come to Washington frequently on weekends. As inspector general, I would be responsible for visiting the

Frankie with U.S. president Jimmy Carter, 1979.

ten regional CSA offices; Missouri is in Region 7, so whenever I had to visit the Missouri office in Kansas City, I would stop off in St. Louis.

The next question had to do with my staff. As I looked into this, I discovered that the CSA Office of Inspector General (OIG) would have eighteen investigators and twenty-three auditors; they and their support staff were all transferred to the OIG. But I myself was not provided with any administrative staff, and I knew I would need one assistant to head the team of auditors, another to head investigations, and a third to handle the operation of the audits. I also needed a counsel of my own, and of course I needed a secretary. I pulled together a budget for all of this, and Senator Eagleton arranged for an additional appropriation to cover it.

The Confirmation Hearings

Next I met with the CSA director and his staff, and they all assured me of their full cooperation. Then in April, the president established an executive group of the prospective inspectors general, and I began attending those sessions, where we exchanged information on how to develop prevention programs.

My confirmation would occur in two stages. The first hearing took place before the Senate's Committee on Labor and Human Resources on July 18, 1979. In advance, I had made the usual courtesy visits to committee members, including Senator Eagleton; the chairman, Harrison A. Williams, Jr., of New Jersey; Jacob Javits of New York; Orrin G. Hatch of Utah; Alan Cranston of California; Howard Metzenbaum of Ohio; Claiborne Pell of Rhode Island; and Edward M. Kennedy of Massachusetts. At the hearing, only Senators Williams, Eagleton, and Javits were present, and Senator Eagleton introduced me to the committee.

My friend and chairman of the U.S. Commission on Civil Rights, Arthur Flemming, had accompanied me to this hearing, and he later made a statement on my behalf. Senator Javits had already said that he supported my confirmation; however, when he saw Dr. Flemming, Senator Javits added that "I was for her anyhow, but if you are for her, I certainly am for her."

Frankie with U.S. president Jimmy Carter and his wife, Rosalynn, August 24, 1979.

Frankie hugs Judge Constance Baker Motley, who administered the swearing-in oath; husband Shelby is on left. October 1979.

I spoke next, saying that I knew the CSA had made some progress in its mission to be a strong advocate for the poor. "However," I added, "some of the programs have been subject to abuse and waste." And I went on to say that:

> The identification of all poor people, the fair and wise allocation of resources, the training for human development and meaningful participation of poor people in community action and economic development programs require continuous and persistent assessment and monitoring. We have an obligation to institute and maintain controls and safeguards to assure efficiency in management and operation at all levels.

On September 20, I met successfully with the Senate Committee on Governmental Affairs, and then on October 4, 1979, I was finally confirmed for the office of inspector general. Judge Constance Baker Motley, with whom I had remained friends ever since we worked together

Friends and family gather in Washington, D.C., for Frankie's swearing in as the first inspector
general of the Community Services Administration (an anti-poverty agency), October 1979.

on the *Davis* case, presided at my swearing-in ceremony at the CSA offices.
My whole family was there to watch, and it was a wonderful occasion.

Work as Inspector General

As soon as I was confirmed by the Senate, I submitted my resignation
to the Civil Rights Commission, effective upon the confirmation of my
successor. But Mary Frances Berry, who later became chair of the commission, was not confirmed until July 7, 1980—so for nine months after I
took office as inspector general, I served concurrently as a commissioner.
When I finally stepped down, President Carter wrote me a letter of
thanks, which I still cherish.

Moving into the inspector-general position, I began by appointing
my administrative staff: Eileen Seidman as deputy inspector general;
Cassandra Menoken as counsel to the OIG; Allen Gibson as assistant
inspector general for investigation; Joseph Kratz as assistant inspector
general for audit; and Lucy Harrison as staff assistant to the OIG.

Our offices were on the fourth floor of the CSA headquarters at Nineteenth and M Street Northwest.

Already, we had heard rumors about political use of CSA funds. In Philadelphia, there were reports that the mayor's office was bypassing the election board and squeezing out people to make room for patronage appointments. In West Virginia, an employee had allegedly leased a car and bought insurance, using CSA funds for personal matters. So we set to work immediately.

The CSA had been established by the Head Start, Economic, and Community Partnership Act of 1974 as the successor to the Office of Economic Opportunity. Its purpose was to reduce poverty in America by using federal, state, and local funds to establish community-action programs, overseen by local boards, that would help the poor help themselves out of poverty by providing them with economic and educational opportunities. Overall, the CSA, which had a budget of more than $600 million, consisted of 888 community-action agencies in every state and ten regions around the country; the Human Development Corporation in St. Louis was one of them.

Like all federally assisted programs, the CSA was subject to regular audit, and the OIG was supposed to ensure that the CSA's agencies were complying with regulations. Joseph Kratz and his staff were responsible for reviewing accounting records and internal controls; Allen Gibson and his group investigated complaints relating to fraud, mismanagement, or other violations of rules and regulations. We had weekly meetings in which Mr. Kratz and Mr. Gibson would report on what they had found. In the case of a possible criminal matter, we sent it on to the Justice Department for prosecution.

In each federal agency, the OIG was required to make semiannual reports to Congress, describing what had taken place over the previous six months. My first report, dated May 30, 1980, covered my activities during the first half of the 1980 fiscal year: organizing the office; hiring the senior staff, including an attorney who reported to me; training those staff members; visiting all ten regional offices; establishing or revising OIG policies; and instituting more stringent auditing and investigation procedures.

My staff and I also had begun to identify some of the agency's more obvious problems, ordering a review of its contract-procurement practices. During fiscal year 1979, for example, CSA awarded thirty-two contracts totaling a little more than $3 million, but our review showed that 98 percent of them were awarded on a noncompetitive basis and that 70 percent were awarded during the last month of the fiscal year. We also found a strong need for competition among firms that were awarded contracts under the Small Business Act. To remedy these situations, we recommended that the CSA reestablish the requirement that all contracts be awarded on a competitive basis and develop new policies for Small Business Act contracts.

By the time of my second report, dated November 28, 1980, we had begun to clarify and strengthen our role. During that period, we responded to eighteen congressional requests for information, and I personally attended or testified at five congressional hearings. Our auditing staff issued 823 reports and questioned $11.7 million in costs to grantees ranging from $21 in one report to $1.8 million in another. Altogether, we disallowed $4.4 million of those costs.

Out of the cases we pursued during that period, our investigations led to nine indictments and six convictions. For example, in one investigation of alleged fraud and kickbacks at the Greater Los Angeles Community Action Agency, there were sixteen counts of false statements, four of conspiracy, eight of bribery, four of theft of federal funds, two of aiding and abetting, and one each of obstruction of justice and filing a false tax return. Another involved the Bergen County Community Action Program in Hackensack, New Jersey. A series of articles had appeared in a local newspaper alleging misuse of government funds and kickbacks; the CSA regional director asked for an investigation by the OIG, and three congressmen also requested an audit. Our investigation resulted in the firing of one employee and the reorganization of the grantee's board of directors.

We also established a hotline, which we publicized in all our regional offices, so that people who had complaints could quickly report them. Hotline calls triggered several important investigations and alerted us to problems. During the period covered by our second report, we received fifty-two complaints, including charges of conflict of interest, fraud

Frankie (second row, last on right) at the U.S. Inspectors General Conference in Charlottesville,
Virginia, 1980.

against the government, mismanagement, and kickbacks. At the same time, we made sure that "whistle-blowers" did not suffer because they had stepped forward to complain. In the case of one employee who had been terminated because of a complaint, we got the person reinstated. But, as things turned out, we had little time for more accomplishments.

Fired—Again

I had always had a warm regard for President Carter. Shelby and I had attended his inauguration, and as a member of the Civil Rights Commission, I had met regularly with him, his staff counsel, Bob Malson, and Martha "Bunny" Mitchell, who was a member of the president's domestic policy staff and later became a senior vice president of Fleishman-Hillard in St. Louis.

In November 1980, a little more than a year after I became inspector general, Ronald Reagan was elected president. Shortly after the election, the inspectors general had a meeting at the White House with the counsel to President Carter, and we asked whether we should submit our resignations to the new administration. We were told that President Carter had said our positions were outside of politics and we did not need to resign.

President Reagan was inaugurated on January 20, 1981. On January 21, around 4 P.M., I received a call from William Allison, the administrator of CSA. I went to his office on the fifth floor, and he handed me an envelope from the White House. Inside was a letter from E. Pendleton James, an assistant to the president, informing me that I had been dismissed as inspector general effective the day *before*, along with the other fourteen inspectors general. It was a great shock. As I said later to a reporter, "The language of the law creating the job of inspector general expressly says the position is to be filled 'without regard to political affiliation.'"

By the time I got back to my office on the fourth floor, everybody knew what had happened. The first thing I did was ask my secretary whether I had signed any reports that day, because if I had, they were invalid. However, January 20 had been a holiday in Washington, and nothing had taken place; in fact, many of the other inspectors general had used the day to visit regional offices—but something had told me to stay in town. I was glad about that, since I had to close my office quickly and clear things out.

Soon the news spread. On January 22, Senator Eagleton—who was the ranking minority member on the Senate Committee on Governmental Affairs—wrote a letter to the president expressing his strong concern about this decision, saying that he feared "an indiscriminate removal of all inspectors general will inflict a real setback in the battle against fraud and waste." In the midst of the furor over these firings, President Reagan said his intentions had been misunderstood, that the inspectors were invited to reapply for their jobs, and that his staff would carefully consider those who wanted to remain. Meanwhile, I was asked to stay on as a consultant to the CSA.

My response was "No!" Some Republican friends, Howard and Elaine Jenkins—he was a professor at Howard law school and had been assistant secretary of labor—called me after seeing one of the newspaper articles and urged me to reapply. I said, "No way. I am going back to St. Louis." I

Members of the NAACP at a tribute for Frankie in St. Louis at the Chase-Park Plaza Hotel, August 1979.

did not want to be associated with an administration that would do business in this way. It was just plain gross. I also felt that even if I did reapply and get my job back, I would have to be prepared to kowtow to the administration—and I was not going to do that. Other people did reapply, saying, "I wish I were in the position to refuse, but I have to work." Well, I had to work too, but I did not have to stay there.

In one newspaper article, an administration spokesman was quoted as saying the administration was looking for inspectors general who were "meaner than a junkyard dog" when it came to ferreting out waste and mismanagement. I told a reporter who called me about this statement that "I don't fit those qualifications." However, our old friend, Charles Oldham, said to me privately, "Frankie, oh yes you do!"

Chapter Nine

Home Again

1981–present

I N 1981 I CAME BACK TO ST. LOUIS, where I felt very welcome. The *St. Louis Post-Dispatch* had written an editorial, "Unqualified as a Junkyard Dog," which condemned my firing as inspector general of the Community Services Administration, and I had a lot of community support. My church even had a welcome-home party for me.

I was hurt by what had happened, and it took me a while to get over it. But I did, and I got to where at least I could talk about it. Shelby always felt differently about these kinds of things. If someone asked me for something and I agreed, he might remind me about what he or she had once done or said about me. He would say, "Don't you remember? Why would you do that?" He was surprised that I didn't hold a grudge, but I just can't be bothered with it. If you hold on to something, it hurts so that you can't continue—and I needed to move on.

One thing that helped was that I knew I could return to the law firm I had left, so at least I did not have to worry about finding a job. But I was turning sixty-five in 1981, and I decided that I would apply for federal retirement benefits. With this income, I could practice law in an "of counsel" position, not as a partner, which meant fewer hours at work. For about six months, I served part-time as the city attorney for Wellston, then resigned to become an adjunct assistant professor at the University of Missouri–St. Louis, where I taught a course in administration of justice for several years until I decided to cut back further on my workload. From time to time now, I meet lawyers who were my students then.

They recall the field trips we did, to the prison at Pacific, Missouri, the city jail, and so on.

Among my own cases during this period was one that involved a civilian employee, Laurine Stimage, an African American woman who worked at the Federal Records Center in St. Louis. She had filed a grievance charging that she had been denied promotion because of racial discrimination; she also brought that grievance to the attention of the NAACP, and Ina Boon, a friend of mine who was regional director for the NAACP, contacted me to represent Ms. Stimage at the hearing. It was resolved in her favor—she got the promotion.

Another case had a higher public profile. On August 2, 1982, the Reverend Jesse Jackson and his Chicago-based organization, Operation PUSH, announced in St. Louis that they would be targeting Anheuser-Busch Companies in an effort to work out a trade agreement with the company that would give a larger share of business to blacks. Afterward,

Frankie in her office at Montgomery Hollie and Associates with a portrait of Martin Luther King, Jr., on the wall behind her, 1986.

at a meeting with about one hundred black St. Louis businessmen, Reverend Jackson requested a contribution of $500 from each one to become members of the economic arm of PUSH, which had won such trade agreements in the past from Seven-Up Company and others. Some people understood him to be implying that they could not share in any potential benefits from his trade agreements unless they contributed.

On August 5, an editorial in the *St. Louis Sentinel,* an African American newspaper, was headlined "Reverend Jesse Jackson: Minister or Charlatan?" It described Jackson as "infamous" and "self-serving" and accused him of taking a "'kick-back' approach to the Black Community." It also defended the brewery, saying that Anheuser-Busch "has led the way for 'Corporate America' in attempting to give something back to the Black Community." Reverend Jackson demanded an apology from the newspaper, which it refused to give.

So, on August 20, 1982, Reverend Jackson and Operation PUSH filed suit in the U.S. District Court for the Eastern District of Missouri against the *Sentinel* and its publisher, Jane Woods. The plaintiffs alleged damage to their stature and good name and said that the editorial had hampered their ability to acquire funding for various programs. They sought $1.5 million in damages on behalf of Reverend Jackson and another $1.5 million on behalf of Operation PUSH, together with attorneys' fees and costs. Reverend Jackson was quoted as saying that "the most basic point is the falsity of the charge that we are trying to extort money." In a different article, Jane Woods said that Reverend Jackson had offered to drop his suit entirely if she would print a retraction, but she would not do so.

Instead, she retained me to represent her and the *Sentinel.* After my motion to dismiss was denied, I filed an answer on behalf of the defendants and, shortly thereafter, a request for the production of documents relating to the financial affairs of Operation PUSH. I also filed notice to take depositions from Reverend Jackson and Richard Hatcher, mayor of Gary, Indiana, and chairman of the board of PUSH. After several delays and the failure of the plaintiffs to respond, I filed a motion on August 9, 1983, to compel the depositions of Reverend Jackson and Richard Hatcher and, if they continued to refuse, an order to dismiss the plaintiffs' petition with payment of attorney's fees.

On August 19, Judge William Hungate issued an order requiring the plaintiffs to produce their documents no later than ten days from the date of the order; it also required Reverend Jackson to appear for deposition on or before September 19, 1983. But on September 14, attorneys for Reverend Jackson and Operation PUSH filed memoranda dismissing the suit, with prejudice, at the plaintiffs' cost. The matter was at an end. At about the same time, Reverend Jackson ended his dispute with Anheuser-Busch. He was quoted as saying that the differences between PUSH and the brewery "may have been attributable to a failure of communication."

I was glad the litigation had ended because I could think of no justification for Reverend Jackson to continue; individuals in other communities had raised concerns about his "trade agreements" that were similar to those expressed in the *Sentinel*. But neither of us treated each other differently after the suit was concluded. I had a cordial relationship with Jesse Jackson before his suit was filed, and we still have a cordial relationship.

Back into Civil Rights

The summary dismissal of all the inspectors general was the first indication of trouble during the Reagan administration—and that was just the beginning. During this period, all the former commissioners were on the phone a great deal talking about something that troubled us deeply: the administration's position on civil rights.

In 1981, after nine years of service, Dr. Flemming was dismissed from the Civil Rights Commission because of disagreements with the administration. Then commissioners Mary Frances Berry, Murray Saltzman, and Blandina Ramirez were also dismissed. The two women filed suit, and eventually Mary Frances Berry was reinstated; today she is the commission's chairperson. Clarence Pendleton, a conservative Republican who had originally come out of the Urban League movement, was named in Dr. Flemming's place. When he was first appointed, he visited St. Louis and I had a reception for him, to which many civil rights leaders came. Afterward, once his conservative position was pretty well known, I thought to myself, "Well, that's the end of *that*."

On the day he was dismissed, Dr. Flemming said publicly that the Reagan administration was moving back toward a "separate but equal" philosophy in school-desegregation cases. Then in December 1981, I received a letter from him that began, "Dear Frankie, I am writing to share with you my deep concern about retrogressive measures that the federal government is taking in civil rights." He mentioned, for example, the administration's attempts to rescind affirmative-action policies and said that "major attention should be directed to the fact that current policies are closing *all* of the doors that have been opened to minorities and poor people in recent years." He suggested that we form a new group to oppose these actions and stand up for what we believed in.

I called him as soon as I got the letter and said, "I'm on board." At that point, we contacted others, including William Taylor, the former staff director of the Civil Rights Commission; Theodore Hesburgh, Manuel Ruiz, Murray Saltzman, and Erwin Griswold, former commissioners; William Brown, Eleanor Holmes Norton, and Aileen Hernandez, past members of the Equal Employment Opportunity commission; Ray Marshall, former secretary of labor; Birch Bayh, former U.S. senator; Elliot Richardson, former U.S attorney general; Harold Tyler, former deputy attorney general; and William Marutani, another former federal official. We were a bipartisan group, and all of us were committed to ending racial discrimination and devising remedies—in such areas as housing, employment, education, and voting—that would counteract its harmful effects. Our role would be to monitor civil rights enforcement, study policies that affect equality of opportunity, alert officials to our concerns, and release reports. We had our first meeting on July 19, 1982, and decided to call ourselves the Citizens' Commission on Civil Rights.

A few days after that meeting, Dr. Flemming received a call from President Reagan about the importance of implementing civil rights laws. That was the kind of person President Reagan was: personable, affable. His position was that he agreed absolutely with civil rights but thought the government should not be doing it all, that it should also involve the states or the private sector. It appeared to us, however, that his administration wanted to *stop* enforcing the federal civil rights laws, reversing a trend that had begun in the late 1940s under President Harry S Truman.

We were also concerned about what was happening to the Civil Rights Commission under the Reagan administration. In July 1983, nine of us former commissioners, including all three former chairmen, called on Congress to block the administration's efforts to interfere with the commission's long-standing tradition of independence. At that time, the administration either had removed or was intending to remove a majority of the commissioners, subject the commission's reports to scrutiny by the Office of Management and Budget, and appoint as staff director a person the commissioners themselves had rejected. In a press release, we said: "In its twenty-five-year history, the commission has not been the handmaiden of either political party." That September, a conference of the chairpersons of all the state advisory committees also issued a resolution saying that the removal of these commissioners was "unprecedented and endangers the historic independence and integrity of the commission."

These times also affected me personally. While I was on the Civil Rights Commission, I had stayed in touch with the Missouri State Advisory Committee by occasionally suggesting names of possible members: Ruth Jacobsen of Fleishman-Hillard, for example, and Anita Bond, who became its chairman. After leaving the commission, I had been invited to rejoin the committee myself and was named its chairman in 1983; we were active during this time, holding community forums and issuing reports on affirmative action, contract compliance, and federal civil rights enforcement efforts. Among the black leaders who served with me during this period were Henry Givens, Jr., of Harris-Stowe College, and John B. Ervin, who was then vice president of the Danforth Foundation. But in the conservative climate that prevailed early in 1985, I received a letter from the committee thanking me for my services but indicating that they would no longer be needed—a cause of unhappiness for me, but not really a surprise.

However, the Citizens' Commission remained active all this time, and during the 1980s we issued reports on school desegregation, housing, affirmative action, and voting. One major report, "One Nation Indivisible," published in 1989, consisted of forty papers prepared by scholars and practitioners who responded to our invitation to look closely at the federal record on enforcement of civil rights laws. These analyses showed that government civil rights practices during the 1980s repre-sented a dramatic break with those of past administrations, both

Democratic and Republican. The Reagan administration, we said, had moved away from bipartisan efforts to eliminate discrimination in American society. Now it would take a large-scale rebuilding effort within the government to assure that people who were denied equality of opportunity receive tangible assistance.

Another bitter disappointment came when President George H. W. Bush vetoed the Civil Rights Act of 1990. He lost the opportunity to set the nation on a course toward progress and reconciliation and instead chose to ignore the deep-seated divisions that threatened the strength and unity of the nation. On the other hand, we felt that President Bill Clinton's election presented a new opportunity for realizing some goals in the area of equal opportunity, and a new momentum was possible. I also liked the civil rights record of his cabinet and judicial appointees and knew some of them personally. In one report, the Citizens' Commission said that the Clinton administration had made a good beginning in its efforts to restore federal civil rights performance. For instance, its early actions included passage of the National Voter Registration Act and the Family and Medical Leave Act, as well as the issuance of executive orders

Frankie greets President George H. W. Bush, both having received honorary degrees from Hampton University at the commencement ceremony, May 1991.

Frankie greets U.S. president Bill Clinton, 1994. The president was one of the speakers for the national conference of the National Council on the Aging.

to address fair-housing and environmental-justice issues. However, our report also identified challenges faced by the administration because of resistance from the Republican majority in Congress.

Today, the Citizens' Commission is still very much in existence, releasing reports on such issues as affirmative action and magnet schools. One of them, from February 2002, "Rights at Risk—Equality in the Age of Terrorism," included twenty papers by experts who analyzed the dangers to civil rights across the spectrum of social and economic policy. As the George W. Bush administration wages a vigorous war on terrorism, it is neglecting civil rights enforcement. Our report states that, while the Citizens' Commission fully understands national imperatives and supports the bipartisan manner in which Congress has addressed the fallout from the September 11, 2001, attacks, the basic rights that many Americans have taken for granted and the democratic principles that have drawn so many to this country are gravely at risk. The commission forwarded its findings to the White House in hopes of stimulating a reconsideration of administration policies.

Aging Issues

Race and gender have both been important issues in my life, but it was only during my latter years on the Civil Rights Commission, when we were holding hearings on age discrimination, that I began to see myself as part of this group. I began to realize that age had become a factor in my case when a national newspaper story appeared in 1979 about my appointment as inspector general. The story said that two African Americans had been appointed and that one of them was "a grandmother." That was *me*. The writer did not see me as a lawyer, or as a woman with a background in civil rights, but as an older person. I think the reporter was actually amazed—like when people sometimes say to me now, "Oh, you look so good." They aren't really surprised that I look so *good*, they are just surprised that I am still walking around.

It also hit me that I was older when I returned to St. Louis and decided that I would be willing to serve on a corporate board. I had my résumé reviewed by Elliot Stein, a headhunter for such boards, who told me that it was impressive—but I was too old. I was sixty-four, and this was the first time that my age had defined what I could be. It was a disappointment, but there was nothing I could do about it; people have a right to choose their board. However, my brother Andy said he believed that my years on the Civil Rights Commission had disqualified me for any of these boards, that I would be considered a possible troublemaker.

Actually, I had already been interested in issues related to aging for several years, and not just as a commissioner. In 1978, Arthur Flemming, who was then U.S. Commissioner on Aging, told me that he was recommending me as a board member of the National Council on the Aging (NCOA). Jack Ossafsky, the executive director, also called and sent me some material. I began to feel this was something I ought to do, but I still thought the NCOA was an organization made up mostly of older people. So my first shock was going to a meeting in Washington, D.C., and discovering that the board included people who worked with the aging or were committed to eliminating age discrimination but were not, for the most part, older adults themselves. I also realized that Dr. Flemming had nominated me because he was very sensitive to the omission of African Americans—and this board was predominantly

The National Council on the Aging Board of Directors, 1997. Frankie is third from left in front row.

white. When I attended that first meeting I thought to myself, "Oh, *this* is why he got me here!"

I had never before recognized how many issues there are in the field of aging, and soon I became very involved in them. Members include senior centers, area agencies on the aging, adult day care centers, senior housing, health centers, and employment services—the NCOA deals with issues related to all these areas. It was fascinating to learn about things that happen to older adults, both good and bad. For example, many senior workers face age discrimination or even termination, but others find unexpected opportunities. In one case, an elite ladies' clothing store told us it had started employing older women because they came to work on time and never called in with babysitter problems.

As part of my role on the NCOA board, I worked to make sure that nationally there was inclusiveness and representation. I wondered, for example, why providers who came to our conventions were mostly white, and I was told that it is expensive to attend and minority providers might not have the necessary budget. So the NCOA found resources to subsidize more minorities and make its conventions more inclusive. In other words, the public-policy themes that I had been working with at the Civil Rights Commission also became the themes that I worked with in relation to the NCOA.

My interest in problems related to aging also led to other assignments. I served briefly as a member of the American Bar Association's Commission on Legal Problems for the Elderly, reviewing and developing durable power of attorney related to health care and other documents to protect the elderly. I also chaired a workshop at a United Nations conference, cosponsored by the NCOA, celebrating the "Year of the Older Person."

In my own life, I have found that the senior years are wonderful if you can accept the fact of aging and enjoy both what you have accomplished and what you still can do. At this stage of life, we miss so much if we don't interact with others. My friends cross all generations; we learn from one another, and that energizes me. Of course I get tired, but I don't expect to be able to do what I did when I was younger—you shouldn't be afraid to say that you are tired because you are old. There are also times when I go into a different room and wonder, "What did I come in here for?" But actually I feel pretty good, and I am grateful for this time in my life.

Girl Scouts and Illness

During the years when I was getting involved with the NCOA, I was also becoming involved with the Girl Scouts—I don't know of any group that does more for girls. I came to this membership in a roundabout way. After I moved to St. Louis, the first not-for-profit board I served on was the League of Women Voters; contacts I made there led to a board position with the YWCA, which led in turn to the board of the Girl Scout Council of St. Louis. In 1978, I was elected to the national board of the Girl Scouts of the USA and remained on it for twelve years.

In 1987, I was thrilled to serve as a delegate to the world conference of Girl Scouts and Girl Guides in Kenya—but my trip was unexpectedly cut short. Our delegation had arrived in Nairobi a week before the world conference was due to begin, and Peter and Muthoni arranged for us to have some special experiences, such as visiting a day-care center owned by

Frankie with Girl Scouts of the USA executive director Frances Hesselbein (far right) at the world conference of Girl Scouts and Girl Guides in Nairobi, Kenya, 1987.

Muthoni, where the seventy children put on a show for us. Then, on the third day of the conference, I got a call from my grandson Terry that Shelby had had a second heart attack. His first attack had happened in May 1986 while we were on our way home from a short vacation in Kimberling City, Missouri, and he had recovered well that time. He was able to resume teaching on the computer-science faculty of the State Community College in East St. Louis.

When this second attack happened, the Girl Scout staff took care of me right away, getting me on a plane to London and back to St. Louis, all by the next day. As soon as I got home, someone hurried me over to the hospital. After a while Shelby was up and about again, but he was less active this time and had to retire from teaching. Fortunately, we have always had good health insurance so at least we were able to have some help over the following weeks and months. If I had to travel, I had a friend or a nurse stay with him. He was never, ever, left alone.

Frankie greets First Lady Nancy Reagan, honorary president of Girl Scouts of the USA, during the celebration of the organization's seventy-second anniversary, 1984.

Frankie, as vice president of Girl Scouts of the USA, greets First Lady (and thus honorary president of Girl Scouts) Barbara Bush at the White House, 1989.

Frankie (top row, third from right) and Shelby (second row, in print shirt) enjoy a Freeman family picnic on Waterman Place, 1986.

However, Shelby had another heart attack in January 1988—and this time his health really began to decline. Over five years he had six heart attacks all together. Once I was in Washington at an NCOA board meeting, and someone asked about Shelby. She said, "Well, Frankie, you know you are a caregiver." I had been talking about the problems of aging and about caregivers, but it was only then that I identified myself as a caregiver. She also said, "Now you be sure to take care of yourself, too." As a caregiver, you forget to take care of yourself, and you *need* to do that; I am sensitive to that now and tell other people the same thing.

One thing that helped during this period was the strength of our marriage and the love and support of our daughter and other family members. We were blessed. Of course, there were also times when Shelby and I disagreed with each other—but we always said that was why we had a big house! We had our own space when we wanted it.

In 1990, I was elected a delegate for the Girl Scouts at the world conference in Singapore, but when I reviewed the situation, I realized that Shelby's situation was just too tenuous. In addition, if I had to leave the conference suddenly, it would also place a burden on the few delegates who were left. So I declined, and it was just as well. Shelby's condition was deteriorating. He was up and about sometimes, but at other times he was not.

Then in April 1991, Muthoni happened to be in St. Louis, visiting us and her son. I had been invited to Peoria to be the speaker for the annual meeting of the Peoria Urban League on April 23. I traveled there that day and was to leave the next morning. After my speech that night, I received a call from Muthoni that Shelby had had another heart attack. I came back on the next flight. This time Shelby did not come home; the doctors told us that he would not survive this attack. He remained in the hospital until June 10, then was in an extended-care center until July 12. That night I was with him until about 10 P.M., when his cousin, Shelby Barnes, came by and said, "You go on home." Around midnight he called and told me that Shelby was gone. Immediately, I called our friends and neighbors, Cynthia and Ron Thompson; their whole family quickly picked me up and took me out to the care facility. Pat and Ellis arrived shortly therafter.

Shelby's funeral was at Washington Tabernacle Missionary Baptist Church. I had joined that church in 1949, when the pastor was Reverend John E. Nance, a very eloquent speaker and a man deeply involved in the community. Our church has about nine hundred members today; the Reverend Jesse T. Williams, Jr., is the pastor and an outstanding speaker and leader. Shelby had never been a member, but three months before he died, he told me to call Reverend Williams, and he asked to join the church. He said to me, "That's what you always wanted," though I had actually decided to leave him alone about it. But he decided himself, and I was glad that he had.

The night before Shelby's funeral, the members of his fraternity—the Epsilon Lambda chapter of Alpha Phi Alpha—conducted an Omega Omega service, or special last rites. He was also a member of the Royal Vagabonds, who had a program at the funeral home; and the Gateway

Chapter of the Links, of which I am a member, had a Connecting Link memorial service. At the funeral itself, Reverend Williams gave the eulogy, Gentry Trotter and Ida James sang solos, and the Reverends John Doggett and Eddie W. Triplett gave special tributes. Shelby was buried in Calvary Cemetery. When I die, I will join him there.

Our daughter and son-in-law had been coming home regularly, and they returned for the funeral; my brothers and sister also came in turn and spent a few days with me. Someone told me, "Don't make any quick decisions," and I followed that advice, but our family reunion was already scheduled for that summer in Williamsburg, Virginia, so I went to it. At this point, I had some help from Anheuser-Busch vice president Wayman Smith III, a lawyer and Howard law graduate, who is like another child to me; his father, Wayman Smith II, a member of the board of aldermen, a real-estate broker, and a client of mine, was a dear friend. Through Wayman, August Busch had kindly offered us the use of his beautiful apartment in King's Mill, and that's where we stayed—my friends, Ina Boon, Imelda Carper, and I.

Frankie celebrates her eightieth birthday at Washington Tabernacle Missionary Baptist Church.

Through the following five years, I carried on, still practicing law, still serving in my various board positions. In 1996, my eightieth birthday was approaching. Although I did not know it, Pat contacted my friends Pauline Payne, Janice Mosby, Ina Boon, and others; together, they made arrangements with the pastor and church officers for a birthday party during the regular worship service at Washington Tabernacle on Sunday, November 24. They also invited many other friends and associates and warned them that it was to be a surprise. Pat and Ellis arrived in St. Louis a few days before my birthday; Allie and her daughter, Elaine, did too. When it happened, I was knocked for a loop. Pat had apparently tried to contact everyone I knew because when Pastor Williams called on her to come forward, she produced a birthday book more than six inches thick filled with cards and letters, including several hundred greetings from family, friends, and former classmates. Greetings also came from President Jimmy Carter, Governor Mel Carnahan, Congressman William Clay, and all past presidents of Delta and members of the boards and agencies where I worked through the years. What a wonderful surprise, and I had not had a clue!

Other Board Connections

Even though I was never appointed to a corporate board, I have served on the boards of many not-for-profit organizations that I believe in, including the United Way of St. Louis. That came about as a result of my earlier board membership on the Health and Welfare Council of St. Louis, a group that provided social services in the community. The late John B. Ervin, the first African American dean at Washington University, was also a member of that council. When they decided to merge with the United Way (called the United Fund then), I worked on the task force for the transition. However, I also voiced my objection to becoming part of a group that was then made up mostly of white men—so you can imagine what happened. In 1975, I was asked to join the board of the United Way. Now people come on the United Way board and ask how long I have been a member, and I say, "Forever."

Over the years the United Way has come a long way in terms of diversity and inclusiveness. It has learned that its role is not to do things *for* the black community—I call that a "missionary attitude"—but to do things *with* the black community. Under the leadership of Charmaine Chapman, whose talents, skills, and effectiveness were great for St. Louis, the United Way has made an outstanding contribution to the community. And the black community has responded. As part of the African American Leadership Initiative, established by Dr. Donald Suggs, some three dozen African Americans give $10,000 or more to the community each year. I believe that it is important to initiate a partnership with people. In other words, don't keep asking other people to do something for you; do something for yourself, too—and then it is a shared responsibility. If someone can give only $1, that is just as important as someone who gives $10,000. Give *something*.

I am also a board member of the St. Louis Urban League, though I came to it late in my professional life because of my work early on for the NAACP. I was first elected during the leadership of William Douthit, then was invited back under James Buford and elected board chair. One charge sometimes made against civil rights organizations is that they have been male and chauvinistic, but I was the first woman elected to this position, and Jo Ann Harmon, senior vice president of Emerson Electric, succeeded me. The Urban League brings African Americans and whites together in a peer relationship to work for change. According to its bylaws, one-third of its membership must be white, which I think is very important. James Buford is also an excellent administrator, and he has involved the Urban League in reaching out. For example, the Urban League and the YWCA are now working together on the Head Start program to provide for St. Louis children.

I have long admired the National Council of Negro Women (NCNW), founded in 1935 by Mary McLeod Bethune, who was one of my role models. Starting out with little money, she managed to found the Bethune-Cookman College in Daytona Beach, Florida, and eventually become director of negro affairs during the Franklin D. Roosevelt administration. When she founded NCNW, she said, "If you just have your finger up that's one, but if you take your whole hand, then you can do so much more." She believed in people working together. In 1938, when I was living in New York City, I decided I would call her up and ask if I

A Delta Sigma Theta national convention in St. Louis, 1994. Left to right: Dorothy Height, Betty Shabazz, and Frankie.

could pay a short visit. I went to see her, talked to her—and she listened; I don't remember exactly what she said but I felt inspired by her and the opportunity to meet her.

So once I came to St. Louis, I became a life member of NCNW, which is not only a tribute to the vision of Mrs. Bethune but also to the dedication of Dorothy Height. For example, on her ninetieth birthday in 2002, Dorothy decided that she wanted to hold a fund-raiser to retire the debt on the NCNW building on Pennsylvania Avenue in Washington, D.C. Many of her friends contributed, along with celebrities such as Camille Cosby and Oprah Winfrey—and she raised $5 million, which paid off the entire mortgage.

I have also served as a member of the YWCA board in St. Louis and have been invited from time to time to national YWCA meetings to speak about race and gender issues. I am a member of the St. Louis Black Leadership Roundtable, which works to achieve greater participation of black citizens locally in economic, educational, and political decision making. As a charter member of the Gateway chapter of the Links, Inc., I have also served as president and chair of International Trends, a national group of women who are committed to civic, educational, and cultural activities. In support of my desire to do whatever I can to help people attain higher education, for several years I have served as a member of the chancellor's council of the University of Missouri–St. Louis and as a member of the board of trustees of Ranken Technical College.

Crossing Boundaries

For years, I have also been involved with the World Affairs Council of St. Louis. Part of my interest in international affairs has to do with family background. Not only do I have two cousins who married men from Liberia, but my second cousin Julia—whose father, Moses Smith, and my grandfather, Charles Smith, were brothers—was also a student at Hampton when she met a young man who had come from South Africa to study. They married and went back to Durban to live. As their children grew up, they traveled to the United States and stayed with members of my family.

So my interest in the World Affairs Council came naturally. Even before Muthoni joined us in 1961, the council would occasionally ask me to have lunch or dinner with people from Germany, Italy, or Africa. Some years ago, I received a call telling me that a group of forty international visitors would be visiting St. Louis during the Christmas holidays and asking whether I would invite a couple of them for Christmas dinner. Since Shelby and I were having our annual Christmas Eve open house then, I said, "I would like to invite all forty if you will arrange for transportation. We can welcome them, and this will be an opportunity for the guests who come to my home to meet people from other countries." That started it, and we continued to have international visitors join us every year. For a long time, I was a member of the World Affairs Council board and more recently have become a member of the St. Louis sister city organization, called the St. Louis Center for International Relations. I regard all of these connections as a wonderful way to share whatever I can about our country and to learn about others.

I have also tried to reach out across cultural and religious boundaries.

Metropolitan Zoo Museum District board. Left to right: front row—Ruth Truesheim, Frankie (chair), G. Rankin, and K. Marshall; back row—Fred Warmann, Ken J. Rothman, and Monsignor Stika; missing—J. Margulis.

For more than twenty-five years, I have been a member of the African American Jewish Task Force, a group that got its start through the National Conference of Christians and Jews when there was talk about tensions between Jews and African Americans. We all know one another well enough now that there is a comfort level—we can disagree without being disagreeable. One concern I have expressed is that black folks should not be the only ones speaking out when something bad happens in race relations. For example, during the recent controversy about the Ku Klux Klan wanting to clean up a highway in St. Louis, we all got together and issued a statement about free speech: that there is freedom to say things, even things we hate. And I knew the KKK wasn't going to clean up anything anyway; they just wanted the newsprint.

I believe it is important for citizens to be willing to serve as members of state and local boards. In the 1990s Mayor Freeman Bosley, Jr., appointed me to the Metropolitan Zoological Park and Museum District, which provides tax support for the Missouri Historical Society,

Frankie with Missouri governor Mel Carnahan and his wife, Jean, at the Martin Luther King, Jr., celebration, January 1995.

Frankie with Dr. William Danforth after receiving an honorary degree from Washington University, 1994.

Saint Louis Art Museum, St. Louis Zoo, Missouri Botanical Garden, and St. Louis Science Center. I was recently reappointed to another three-year term by Mayor Francis Slay and became the chair. These cultural institutions are essential components in the life of the entire St. Louis metropolitan community.

I also serve with Dr. William Danforth as co-chair of the St. Louis Community Monitoring and Support Task Force, established in the aftermath of the St. Louis school desegregation case. In that case, the U.S. District Court for the Eastern District of Missouri approved a settlement in which the litigants would appoint a task force to monitor the agreement, which would include representatives of the parties, parent groups, the business community, teachers, colleges and universities, and community leaders. This task force was appointed in October 1999 and issued its first report in April 2001. The problems of improved student performance and full equality of opportunity continue to be a challenge to the task force as its work continues.

The city and its contributions to the St. Louis area are often taken for granted and undervalued—but not by me. I live in the city, and I have only lived in the city. Some people feel that there is a better quality of life in the suburbs, but I believe that is wrong. There's a vitality to the city; it is cosmopolitan, exciting. In 2000, when I decided to sell my house on Waterman Place and move to an apartment, I looked for one only in St. Louis City. A lot of people have moved away, but not Frankie Freeman.

Reflections

My life has been blessed with a wonderful husband and a beautiful daughter and her husband, who blessed our family with three sons—my dear grandsons. My own son's death will always be with me, but my grandsons and now my four great-grandsons have filled the void. I am also sustained by so many memories of Shelby and our life together.

One of those wonderful times was a trip that Shelby and I took to Kenya in 1984. He said that as long as we were going to Africa he wanted to stop off in Egypt and see the pyramids, so we did that too. I think about other times, like the lazy Sunday afternoons we spent on the Missouri River with our dear neighbors and friends George and Imelda Carper, who had a houseboat and invited us to come along. Or the backyard barbecues we had: sometimes with relatives, sometimes with friends from the NAACP or other groups that were important to us. Cooking has always been a pleasure to me, and I have loved sharing meals with family members and friends; I believe there is a special value in "breaking bread together." Through the years, we have had wonderful, warm friendships with many people, and I am grateful for them.

My life, like all lives, has been filled with ups and downs. As Langston Hughes said in one of my favorite poems, it hasn't always been a "crystal stair." For example, I have had cancer twice now. In November 1998, I woke up and my neck was swollen, which scared me to death; I went right away to my doctor, Leslie Bond, and soon I was in the hospital for a biopsy. The pathology report showed that the thyroid was cancerous, so two weeks later I was back in surgery to have my thyroid removed. Now I go to an oncologist every three months for tests to make sure the cancer has not recurred.

Then in 2000, I began having trouble speaking—my voice was hoarse, and I did not know why. This time, Dr. Bond referred me to a throat surgeon, who tested me and said that I had a malignant lesion on my vocal cords that would require surgery. So I had surgery that July—and for two weeks afterward, I was not allowed to talk much. My daughter came and stayed with me for two weeks; she said she wanted to keep me off the phone. Now I go back to that doctor every three months too. My faith has helped me through both bouts with cancer. I just say, "Lord, help the doctor, and help me."

The experience of having cancer has also made me realize that I want to do more to enjoy life, so in the last couple of years I have done a few things that I always meant to do. Twice now I have gone on jazz cruises in the Caribbean, and once I have been on a cruise to Alaska. In that respect, I have also been influenced by the example of Daddy Freeman, who worked, worked, *worked* all his life. Often he would say he wanted to do things like travel to California; he was going to do those things "later." But he died before he got the chance.

So I am trying to enjoy life, but I still believe in the things I have always stood for. I strongly feel that we have to keep working hard to fight discrimination and injustice. People sometimes think they can develop one-shot programs to fix things, but you can't solve an ingrained problem by having a single workshop. These things require persistent, continuous effort. You have to *work* at it. Civil-rights laws are meaningless unless they are enforced.

We have made progress in the area of voting rights, though I believe we still have a long way to go. In 1965, when the Voting Rights Act was passed, thousands of minorities were being denied the right to vote. That is not generally the case now; participation in the electoral process has substantially improved, and nationally there are more than eight thousand black elected officials. But the irregularities that occurred in Florida and elsewhere during the 2000 election show that sometimes an individual may cast a vote but that vote may or may not be counted because of race—and that is a serious problem.

We have so many needs as a society. Affirmative action is as necessary now as it ever was. It is *not* preferential treatment; the whole concept of affirmative action is to reach out and affirmatively extend equal opportunity to all persons, without regard to race, creed, gender, age, or sexual orientation. We need better access to health care for everyone; we still have too many uninsured and underinsured. Education is also vitally important, but you can't separate what happens in the classroom from what happens in the home. When a child comes to class and something is clearly wrong, that child may not have had a meal or a proper place to sleep. Children need families—whatever kind they may be—who love and care for one another; they also need parents who encourage them to learn. But we need to provide more funding for education, particularly in our cities, and find a way to solve the continuing problems of segregation in education, caused by racial isolation in housing. The government must also provide help for working people in terms of quality day care.

Many other challenges face us, too. With respect to race, gender, and age, there has been a great deal of progress in terms of discrimination, but there is still discrimination on the basis of equally irrelevant issues, such as sexual orientation. In the area of criminal justice, too, racial inequality is growing as law-enforcement personnel use racial profiling to single out blacks, Hispanics, and now Arabs or Muslims.

My earlier question—"One Nation or Two?"—has changed a little. As the census figures reflect, we are much more diverse than we were, but

Frankie Muse Freeman, 2000.

many people do not appreciate that diversity. So maybe the question is now: "One Nation—or Three or Four?" I think our survival requires that we take pride in our diversity, but we cannot do this unless we get to know one another. As long as we are living in isolation from one another—whether we are Hispanic Americans, Asian Americans, African Americans, or white Americans—we are missing out on so much.

But I am optimistic, absolutely, that we can deal with these issues because I love my country and because the statement "We hold these truths to be self-evident that all men are created equal" is a powerful one. This concept, of the equality of persons, is not just the law of the land. It is part of my Christianity and part of my soul. Life for all of us has changed since the horrors of the September 11, 2001, attacks, but we must carry on. And we know the "trouble don't last always"—God will make a way somehow and we will survive.

I would say to everyone: "Yes, you have ups and downs. Some days are good and some are not." But I also say, "Keep your hand on the plow." Some people have replied that they are not farmers. But I *still* say, in the words of the old Negro spiritual, "Keep your hand on the *plow*."

In so many speeches I have given over the years, I have quoted a poem that my mother sent me long ago. And every time I read it, somebody asks me for a copy:

It Shows on Your Face

You don't have to tell how you live each day
You don't have to say if you work or play
A tried, true barometer serves in the place
So however you live, it shows on your face.

The false, the deceit that you bear in your heart
Will not stay inside, where it first got its start.
For sinew and blood are a thin veil of lace
However you live, it shows on your face.

If you have battled and won in this great game of life
If you feel you have conquered the sorrow of strife
You have played the game fair and you stand on first base
You don't have to tell it, it shows on your face.

If your life is unselfish, if for others you live
Not for what you can get, but for what you can give
If you live close to God in His infinite grace,
You don't have to tell it, it shows on your face.

—Author Unknown

This is what I believe in; this is how I have tried to live. In my space, in my way, in my own time, I did the best I could—and I still try to make a difference. All we can do is do our best. If I fail, I say, "Lord, I'm sorry," and move on. If you fall on your face, you just get up and try again. You keep the faith…and carry on.

Index